BOOK 2

S0-BXV-701

MAPS • GLOBES • GRAPHS

Writer

Henry Billings

Consultants

Gloria Sesso
Dix Hills, New York

Edna Whitfield
St. Louis, Missouri

STECK-VAUGHN
C O M P A N Y

A Division of Harcourt Brace & Company

www.steck-vaughn.com

Acknowledgments

Editorial Director	Diane Schnell
Project Editor	Janet Jerzycki
Design Manager	Rusty Kaim
Electronic Production	UG/GGS Information Services, Inc.
Media Researcher	Claudette Landry
Cover Design	Donna Neal
Cartography	Land Registration and Information Service Amherst, Nova Scotia, Canada
	Gary J. Robinson
	MapQuest.com, Inc.
	R.R. Donnelley and Sons Company

Photography Credits

Cover images courtesy of Cartesia Software; p. 4 ©Superstock; pp. 5, 6, 7(b) ©PhotoDisc; p. 7(a) ©Zuckerman/PhotoEdit

Illustration Credits

Dennis Harms pp. 8, 56, 64, 70, 71, 72, 75; Michael Krone pp. 22, 86, 87; T.K. Riddle pp. 88, 89; Rusty Kaim p. 4

ISBN 0-7398-0978-4

Contents

To The Learner

Maps•Globes•Graphs is a series of three books designed to help you learn the skills necessary for understanding and using maps, globes, and graphs. Since you will be working with maps directly on each page, you will get lots of hands-on experience. You should find this experience helpful when you read road maps, atlases, and a variety of the kinds of charts and graphs you find in newspapers and magazines.

Each of the chapters in this book focuses on one skill. The first eleven chapters deal with map and globe skills. The last chapter focuses on skills needed to read bar graphs, circle graphs, line graphs, and tables.

In addition to the chapters, you will find a few other features in this book. On pages 92–94 are atlas maps of the United States and the world. You may find these as well as the glossary on pages 95 and 96 handy references. On pages 97–100 there is a sample standardized test. This test covers many of the skills in the book. Its main purpose is to familiarize you with a standardized test format. If you are a student, you will probably take a test similar to this one some time in the future. The answer key is on pages 101–106. The answer key provides the answers to all of the questions in this book. Following the answer key are six outline maps of the world that you can use to practice the skills you learn in the units.

As you work through this book, you will take a trip around the world. Enjoy your trip!

Geography Themes

In *Maps•Globes•Graphs* you will learn about some of the tools that scientists use to study **geography**. Geography is the study of Earth, its features, and the ways people live and work on Earth. There are five **themes**, or main topics, to help people organize ideas as they study geography.

The Five Themes of Geography
- Location
- Place
- Human/Environment Interaction
- Movement
- Regions

Location

Location describes where something is found. You can name a location by using its address. Another way you can tell the location of something is by describing what it is near or what is around it. Location helps us learn where a certain lake is found, or how far a person from Maine must travel to get to Idaho.

 Look at this photograph. How would you describe the location of this home?

_____

_____

Place

Place describes the kinds of features that make a location different from any other on Earth. **Physical features** are part of the natural environment. Some physical features are bodies of water, landforms, climate, soil, and plants and animals. **Human features** are developed or made by people. These features can include airports, buildings, highways, businesses, parks, and playgrounds.

The city in this photograph is Minneapolis, Minnesota. As you study the picture, look for physical and human features of Minneapolis.

 Use the physical and human features you find in the photograph and describe Minneapolis, Minnesota.

_____

_____

_____

Human/Environment Interaction

Human/Environment Interaction describes how people affect the environment and how the environment affects people. This theme also explains how people depend on the environment. For example, people depend on the land for good soil to grow crops.

Human/Environment Interaction demonstrates how people adapt to their environment. It explains how people make changes to live in their surroundings.

 How do the people in these photographs adapt to the change of seasons in their climate?

_____

_____

_____

Human/Environment Interaction also considers how people change the environment to meet their needs and wants. Sometimes people change the course of a river to uncover flooded land or to bring water where it is needed.

 Look at the photograph of the dam shown here. How do you think changing the flow of a river's water might affect the plants and animals in the area?

_____

_____

_____

Movement

Movement explains how people, goods, information, and ideas move from place to place. The movement of people from other countries to settle in the United States is one example of movement. Another example is trade. Goods move across the country or around the world through trade. The spread of information and ideas through the Internet is another kind of movement.

Name two ways that people, goods, information, and ideas move from place to place.

_____

_____

_____

Both photographs above show movement. On the line below each picture write **People/Goods** if the picture shows movement of people and goods. Write **Information/Ideas** if the picture shows movement of information and ideas.

Regions

Regions name areas that share one or more features. Physical features, such as landforms, natural resources, or climate can describe regions. Appalachia is a region in the eastern part of the United States defined by its physical feature—the Appalachian Mountains. Human features, such as land use, politics, religion, or language can also describe regions. Regions can be large or small.

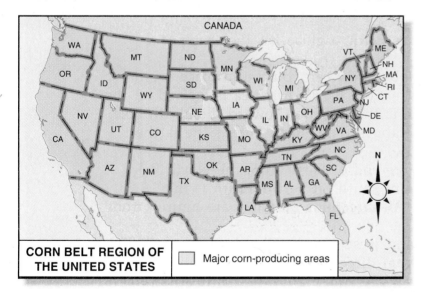

CORN BELT REGION OF
THE UNITED STATES   ☐ Major corn-producing areas

 Look at the map of the United States shown here. List the states that make up the Corn Belt. What makes the Corn Belt a region?

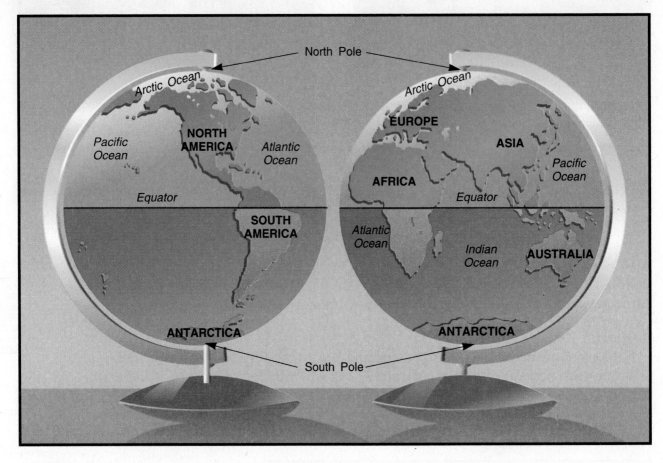

A globe is a model of Earth. Like Earth, a globe has the shape of a sphere, or ball.

The drawing above shows a globe. How can you find a place on the globe? One way is to know its direction. North America is located on the northern part of the globe. North is the direction toward the North Pole. Find the North Pole on the globe above. The **North Pole** is the farthest point north on Earth.

The South Pole is at the opposite end of Earth from the North Pole. The **South Pole** is the farthest point south on Earth. South is the direction toward the South Pole. All directions on Earth are figured from the North and South Poles.

Two other directions are east and west. North (N), south (S), east (E), and west (W) are called the **cardinal directions.** You know that once you are facing north, then east is always to your right. West is to your left. South is behind you. Knowing these directions will help you to find places. Practice using directions on the map above.

► South America is which direction from North America?   South

► The Arctic Ocean is which direction from North America?   North

► The Pacific Ocean is which direction from North and South America?   West

► The Atlantic Ocean is which direction from North and South America?   East

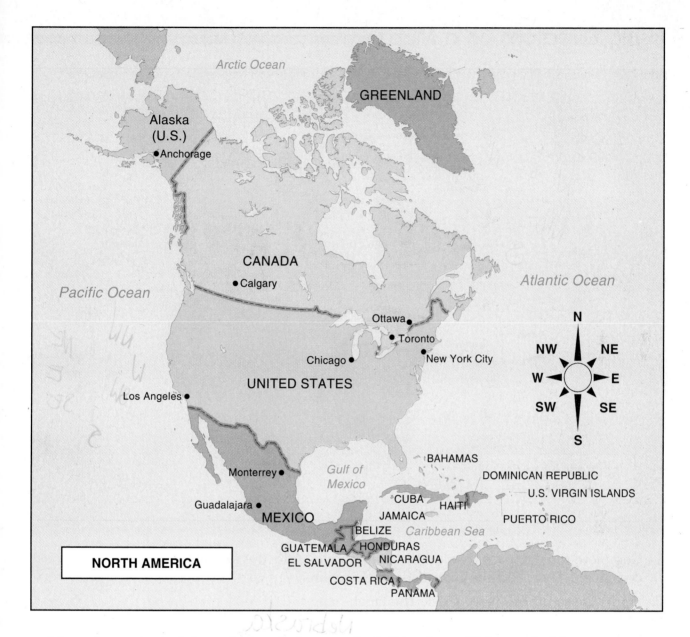

Maps have a special symbol to help you find directions. This symbol is called a **compass rose**. Look at the map above. Find the compass rose. North (N), south (S), east (E), and west (W) are all marked on the compass rose.

There are also other directions on the compass rose. These directions are in between the cardinal directions. They are called **intermediate directions**. The intermediate directions are northeast (NE), southeast (SE), northwest (NW), and southwest (SW). You need these to locate places that are between the cardinal directions

Find Chicago on the map. Find Toronto. What direction is Toronto from Chicago? It is between north and east, or northeast. NE

▶ Find Calgary on the map of North America above. In which direction would you travel from Calgary to reach Anchorage? NW

▶ From Monterrey, what direction is Guadalajara? SW

▶ From Los Angeles, what direction is Monterrey? SE

Using Directions on a Map

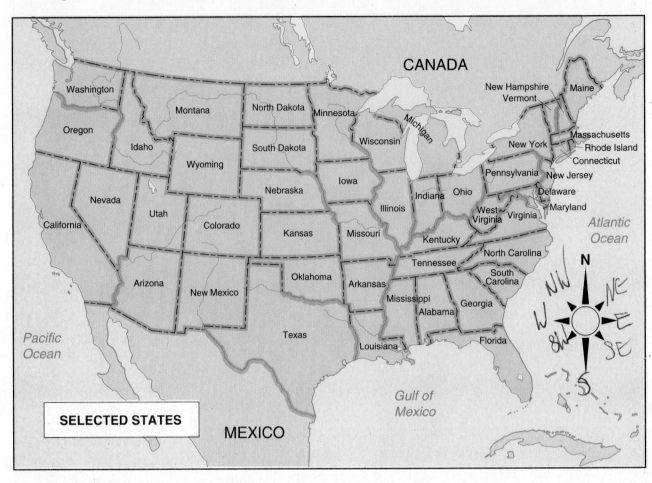

SELECTED STATES

1. Complete the compass rose on the map above. Add the missing cardinal directions. Then add the intermediate directions.

2. Find Kansas on the map. Circle the label.

   a. Which state is north of Kansas? ___Nebraska___

   b. Which state is south of Kansas? ___Oklahoma___

   c. Which state is east of Kansas? ___Missouri___

   d. Which state is west of Kansas? ___Colorado___

3. Which state is northeast of Utah? ___Wyoming___

4. Which state is southeast of Arkansas? ___Mississippi___

5. Which state is southwest of Illinois? ___Missouri___

6. Which state is northwest of Iowa? ___South Dakota___

7. What is west of California? ___Pacific Ocean___

8. What is southeast of Texas? ___Mexico___

Using Directions on a Map

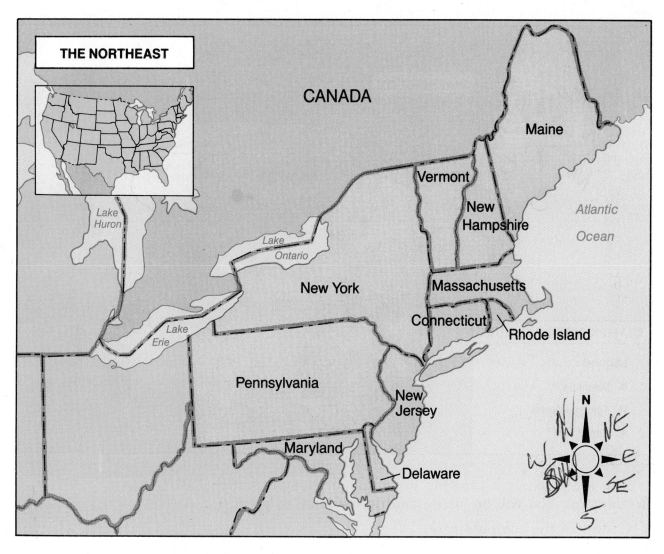

1. Complete the compass rose. First add the cardinal directions. Then add the intermediate directions.

2. Write a direction to make each sentence true.

   a. New Hampshire is _____North_____ of Massachusetts.

   b. Pennsylvania is _____South_____ of New York.

   c. New Jersey is _____South_____ of Connecticut.

   d. New Hampshire is _____North_____ of Rhode Island.

   e. Maine is _____ of New Hampshire.

3. Draw a conclusion. Find the small map of the United States above. It shows where the Northeast region of the United States is located. Why do you think this region is called the Northeast?
   _____Northeastern Sid of North Amura_____

Using Directions on a Map

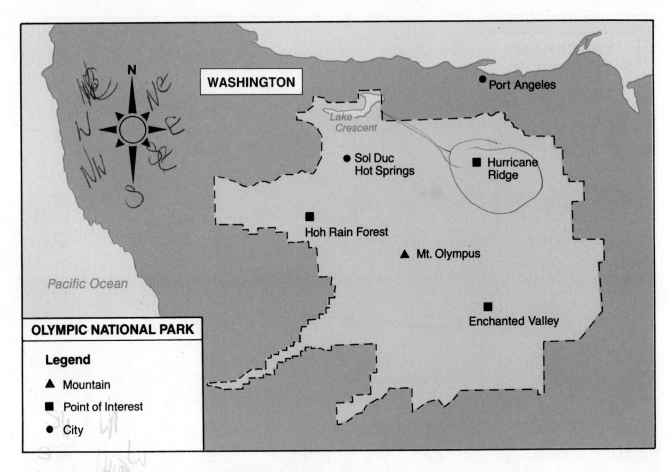

WASHINGTON

Port Angeles

Lake Crescent

Sol Duc Hot Springs

Hurricane Ridge

Hoh Rain Forest

▲ Mt. Olympus

Enchanted Valley

Pacific Ocean

OLYMPIC NATIONAL PARK

Legend

▲ Mountain

■ Point of Interest

● City

You are going on a camping trip through Olympic National Park in Washington. You will be hiking and do not want to get lost.

1. Complete the compass rose.

2. Your trip begins at Hurricane Ridge. It is in the northeast part of the park. Circle it on your map.

   What direction would you look to see Mt. Olympus? ___South___

3. You will hike to Lake Crescent from Hurricane Ridge. What direction will you be walking? ___North West___

4. From Lake Crescent you will hike to Sol Duc Hot Springs. What direction will you be going? ___South___

5. You want to camp in the Hoh Rain Forest. What direction do you hike from Sol Duc Hot Springs to the Hoh Rain Forest? ___South___

6. What direction is the Pacific Ocean from the Hoh Rain Forest? ___West___

7. Your last stop will be at the Enchanted Valley. It is in the southeastern part of the park. What direction will you travel to get back to Hurricane Ridge from the Enchanted Valley? ___North___

Skill Check

Vocabulary Check   **compass rose**   **North Pole**   **intermediate directions**
                        cardinal directions   **South Pole**

Choose from the words above to make each sentence true.

1. North, south, east, and west are the ___Cardinal directions___ .

2. Directions on Earth are figured from the ___North Pole___

   and the ___South Pole___ .

3. Northwest and southeast are two of the ~~Cardinal~~ _Intermediate_ directions .
   on a Compass Rose.

Map Check

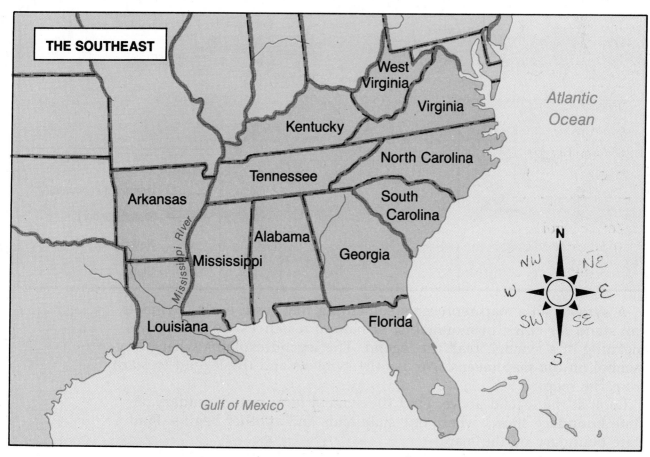

THE SOUTHEAST

1. What state is southwest of South Carolina? ___Georgia___

2. What state is northeast of Kentucky? ___West Virginia___

3. What direction is North Carolina from Tennessee? ___East___

4. What two states are west of the Mississippi River? ___Arkansas___

   and ___Louisiana___

Symbols and Legends

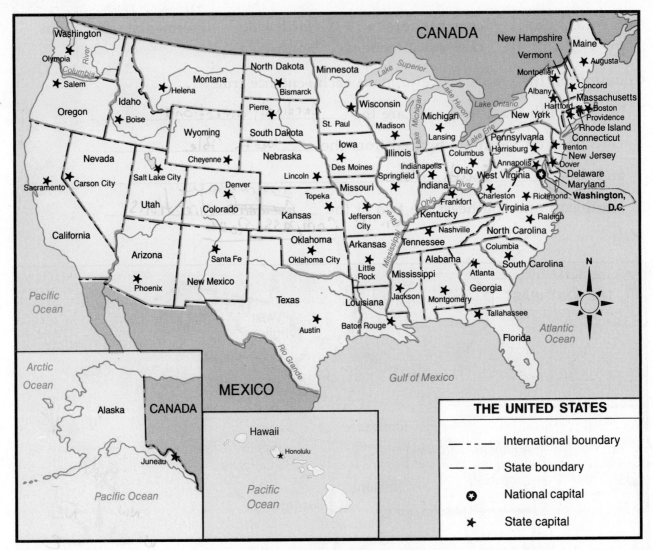

A **symbol** on a map represents something that is on Earth. Symbols can stand for cities, or mountains, or natural resources. To find the meaning of a symbol, read the legend. The **legend** explains what every symbol on the map means. We use the symbols and the legend to learn from the map.

Look at the legend above. Find the symbol for a state boundary. A **state boundary** shows where one state ends and another begins. Find a state boundary on the map.

Find the symbol for an international boundary in the legend. An **international boundary** shows where one country ends and another begins.

▶ Find your state on the map. What is the state capital? Boston
What states border your state? What are their capitals? NH RI CT VT

▶ Does your state have an international boundary? NO
If so, what country shares a border with your state?

▶ What countries border the United States? Canada + Mexico

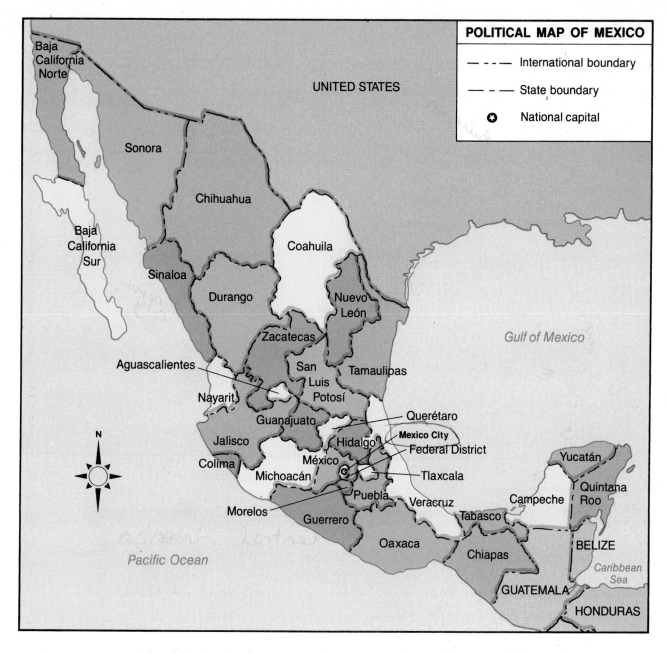

POLITICAL MAP OF MEXICO

- – · – International boundary
- – · – State boundary
- ✪ National capital

UNITED STATES

Baja California Norte

Sonora

Chihuahua

Baja California Sur

Coahuila

Sinaloa

Durango

Nuevo León

Zacatecas

Gulf of Mexico

Aguascalientes

San Luis Potosí

Tamaulipas

Nayarit

Guanajuato

Querétaro

Jalisco

Hidalgo

Mexico City
Federal District

Colima

México

Yucatán

Michoacán

Tlaxcala

Quintana Roo

Morelos

Puebla

Veracruz

Campeche

Guerrero

Tabasco

BELIZE

Oaxaca

Chiapas

Caribbean Sea

Pacific Ocean

GUATEMALA

HONDURAS

N

Some maps show special information about a place. Political maps show the boundaries separating states and countries. Other maps may show yearly rainfall or where people live. That is why the title is so important. The **title** tells you the purpose of the map.

Look at the title of the map above. It is a **political map** of Mexico. What can you expect to learn from this map? You can expect to find capital cities and state and international boundaries. The country of Mexico has 31 states. Like the United States, it has a national capital. Find the symbol for a national capital on this map and on the map on page 14.

► What city is the national capital of the United States? Washington DC

► What city is the national capital of Mexico? Mexico City

► What country touches the northern international boundary of Mexico? USA

► Name two Mexican states along this boundary.
Sonora + Chihuahua

Reading a Political Map

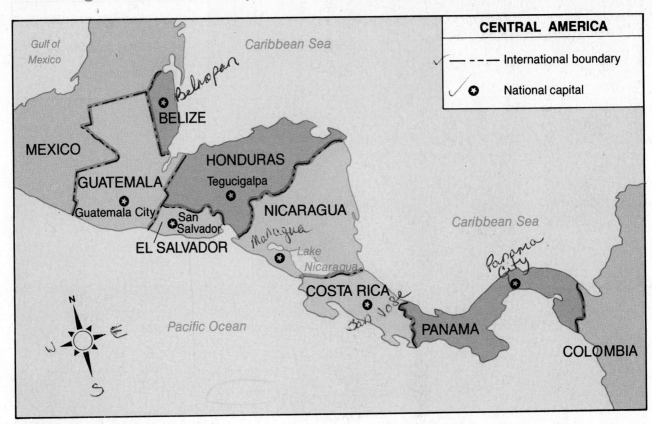

CENTRAL AMERICA

✓ - - - - International boundary

✓ ⊛ National capital

Gulf of Mexico

Caribbean Sea

Belmopan

⊛ BELIZE

MEXICO

GUATEMALA

HONDURAS

Tegucigalpa

⊛

Guatemala City ⊛

⊛ San Salvador

EL SALVADOR

NICARAGUA

Managua

⊛

Lake Nicaragua

Caribbean Sea

Panama City

⊛

COSTA RICA

San Jose

⊛

PANAMA

COLOMBIA

Pacific Ocean

N E W S

MAP ATTACK!

- **Read the title.** This map shows ___Central America___
- **Read the legend.** Check (✔) each symbol after you read its meaning. Check (✔) a matching symbol on the map.
- **Read the compass rose.** Circle the four cardinal directions. Label the intermediate directions.

1. Does this map show states or countries? ___Countries___

   How do you know? ___it's a political map___

2. Trace the borders of Costa Rica in red. What countries share a

   border with Costa Rica? ___Nicaragua + Panama___

3. Write the capital city of each of these countries on the map where it belongs.

   Panama City, Panama   San Jose, Costa Rica
   Managua, Nicaragua   Belmopan, Belize

4. Draw a conclusion. What countries have coastlines on both the Caribbean Sea and the Pacific Ocean?

   _____

   Sonora + Chihuahua

Reading a Political Map

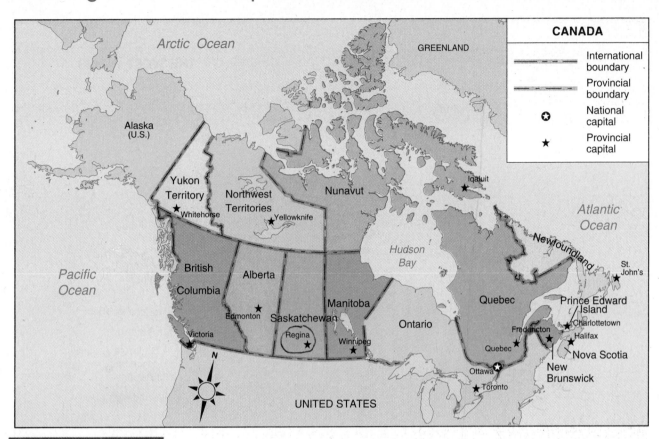

CANADA

———	International boundary
–·–·–	Provincial boundary
✪	National capital
★	Provincial capital

Arctic Ocean

GREENLAND

Alaska (U.S.)

Yukon Territory
★ Whitehorse

Northwest Territories
★ Yellowknife

Nunavut

Iqaluit ★

Atlantic Ocean

Pacific Ocean

British Columbia

Alberta
Edmonton ★

Saskatchewan
Regina ★

Manitoba
Winnipeg ★

Hudson Bay

Ontario

Quebec

Newfoundland

St. John's ★

Prince Edward Island
Charlottetown ★

Fredericton ★
Quebec ★
Halifax ★
Nova Scotia

New Brunswick

Victoria ★

Ottawa ✪
Toronto ★

N

UNITED STATES

MAP ATTACK!

Follow the steps on page 16 to begin reading this map.

1. Canada is divided into ten provinces and three territories. The border lines look like state borders. Why is the border different between

   the Yukon Territory and Alaska? _International border_

2. Circle the capital city of Saskatchewan. Write its name.

   _____ Regina _____

3. Trace the borders of Saskatchewan in red.

   Which province is west of Saskatchewan? _Alberta_

   Which province is east of Saskatchewan? _Manitoba_

4. What is the national capital of Canada? _Ottawa_

5. Halifax is the capital of _Nova Scotia_ .

6. Iqaluit is the capital of _Nunavut_

7. What is the capital of the Northwest Territories? _Yellowknife_

8. What is the capital of the Yukon Territory? _Whitehorse_

Reading a Political Map

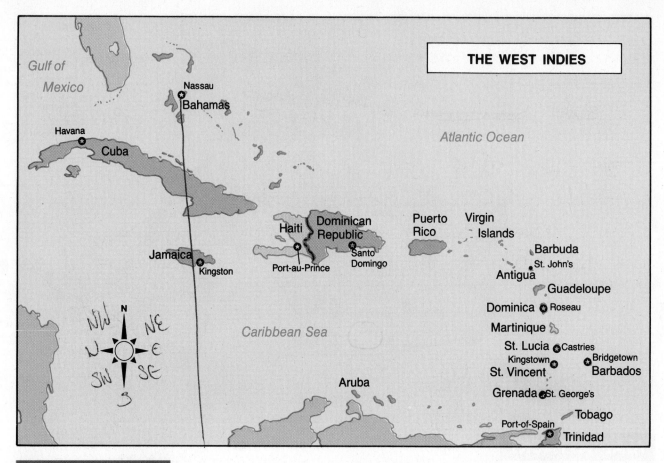

THE WEST INDIES

Gulf of Mexico

Nassau
Bahamas

Havana
Cuba

Atlantic Ocean

Haiti
Dominican Republic
Puerto Rico
Virgin Islands

Jamaica
Kingston
Port-au-Prince
Santo Domingo

Barbuda
St. John's
Antigua
Guadeloupe
Dominica ⊛ Roseau
Martinique
St. Lucia ⊛ Castries
Kingstown
St. Vincent
Bridgetown
Barbados
Grenada ⊛ St. George's
Tobago
Port-of-Spain
Trinidad

Caribbean Sea

Aruba

MAP ATTACK!

Follow the steps on page 16 to begin reading this map.

1. Find the island that is divided into two separate countries. Name each country and its capital.

   a. _____Havana, Cuba_____

   b. _____Santa Domingo, Dominican Republic_____

2. Locate the Bahamas on the map above. Nassau is the capital city of the Bahamas. Draw a line south from Nassau to the bottom of the map.

   What countries do you cross? ___Cuba & Jamaica___

3. Write the intermediate direction that makes each sentence true.

   a. Martinique is ___Northwest___ of Barbados.

   b. Trinidad and Tobago are ___Southeast___ of Puerto Rico.

   c. Guadeloupe is ___Northeast___ of Aruba.

4. Draw a conclusion. The West Indies form the northern and eastern boundary of what sea? ___Caribbean Sea___

Skill Check

Vocabulary Check   **symbol**   **legend**   **title**
                        boundaries   **political map**

Use each word or phrase to finish a sentence.

1. A ~~State~~ ~~boundaries~~ Political Map shows the boundaries that separate different states or countries.

2. The map ___title___ tells you what the map is about.

3. Lines that separate states or countries are ___boundaries___ .

4. The ___legend___ tells you what the symbols on a map mean.

5. A ___Symbol___ on a map can stand for a city, a mountain, or a resource.

Map Check

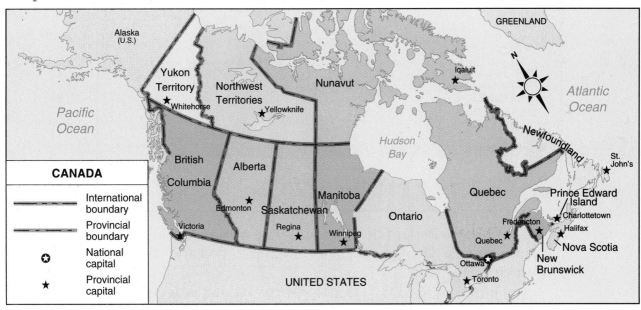

Match the capital with the province.

1. _B_ Toronto   A. Manitoba

2. _E_ Edmonton   B. Ontario

3. _A_ Winnipeg   C. Quebec

4. _C_ Quebec   D. Nova Scotia

5. _F_ Victoria   E. Alberta

6. _D_ Halifax   F. British Columbia

Geography Themes Up Close

Place is a location that has physical and human features that set it apart from other locations. Physical features can include bodies of water, landforms, climate, and plants and animals. Human features can include the kind of government, customs, art, buildings, and other things made by people. The map below shows Florida and some of its features.

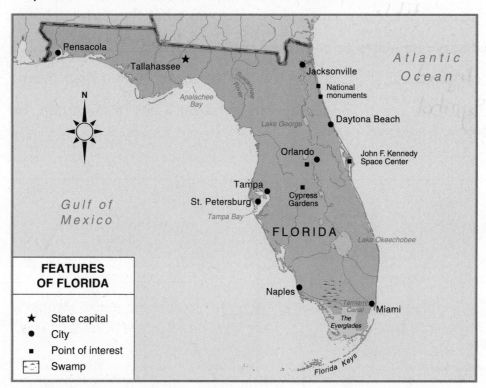

1. Big Cypress Swamp is one physical feature of Florida. This swamp is east of Naples, Florida. Use the symbol for swamp to find and label Big Cypress Swamp on the map.

2. Name three other physical features of Florida shown on the map.

   _____

   _____

   _____

3. The John F. Kennedy Space Center was set up in 1964 as a launch site for space missions. It is on the coast southeast of Daytona Beach. Circle this feature on the map. Then, mark **P** next to the circle if it is a physical feature. Mark **H** if it is a human feature.

4. Walt Disney World, near Orlando, is a human feature of Florida. Use the Point of Interest symbol in the legend to find Walt Disney World. Then, label it on the map.

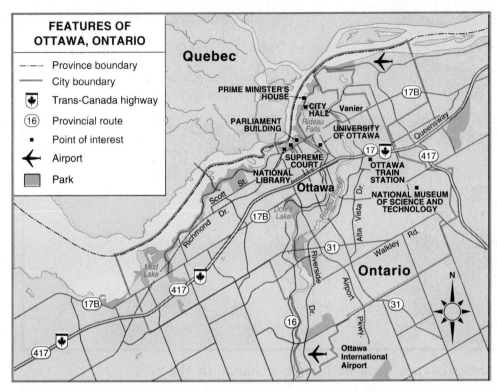

FEATURES OF
OTTAWA, ONTARIO

- – · – · – · Province boundary
- ———— City boundary
- Trans-Canada highway
- (16) Provincial route
- ▪ Point of interest
- ← Airport
- Park

Quebec

PRIME MINISTER'S
HOUSE

CITY
HALL   Vanier

PARLIAMENT   Rideau
BUILDING   Falls   UNIVERSITY
                         OF OTTAWA

(17B)

Queensway

SUPREME
COURT

NATIONAL
LIBRARY

Ottawa

(17)

(417)

OTTAWA
TRAIN
STATION

NATIONAL MUSEUM
OF SCIENCE AND
TECHNOLOGY

Scott   St.

Richmond   Dr.

(17B)

Dow's
Lake

Rideau River

Alta Vista Dr.

Walkley   Rd.

(31)

Mud
Lake

(417)

Riverside

Airport

Ontario

(16)

(31)

Pkwy.

(17B)

(417)

Ottawa
International
Airport

N

5. The Ottawa River forms the northwestern border of Ottawa. Label the Ottawa River. Then, mark **P** next to your label if it is a physical feature. Mark **H** if it is a human feature.

6. Name two physical features of Ottawa. _____

_____

7. The Rockcliffe Airport is a human feature in the northeast corner of Ottawa. Use the airport symbol in the legend to find Rockcliff Airport. Then, label it on the map.

8. What are two other human features of Ottawa?

_____

_____

9. Describe how the features of Ottawa differ from the town or city where you live.

_____

_____

_____

_____

Scale and Distance

A **map scale** compares distance on a map with distance in the real world. We use a map scale to find the distance between two places. A map scale shows distance in both **miles** (MI) and **kilometers** (KM). It looks like this:

```
0        220      440 MI
|----+----+----+----|
0        350      700 KM
```

► What do the letters MI and KM stand for?

► Which distance is longer, 400 miles or 400 kilometers?

Look at the map of the United States on page 23. Suppose you want to find the distance between Los Angeles and New York City. You will need a ruler, a pencil, and a piece of paper.

Here is how you use the map scale.

Step 1 Using your ruler, measure the distance between Los Angeles and New York City. On this map, Los Angeles and New York are 5½ inches apart.

Step 2 Look at the map scale in the lower right-hand corner. You can see that 1 inch equals 440 miles. Remember, there are 5½ inches between Los Angeles and New York City. Use multiplication to find the distance in miles or kilometers.

$$
\begin{array}{rr}
\text{number of miles per inch} & 4\,4\,0 \\
\times \text{ number of inches} & \times\quad 5.5 \\
\hline
= \text{distance in miles} & 2\,4\,2\,0
\end{array}
$$

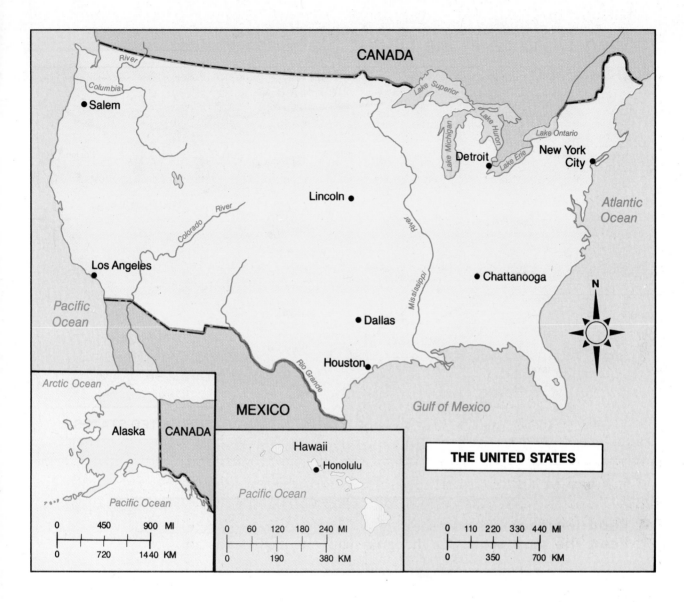

Look at the map of the United States above. Find the two smaller maps in the left-hand corner. One shows Alaska and the other shows Hawaii. Alaska and Hawaii are far from the other forty-eight states. This map isn't big enough to show where Alaska and Hawaii really are. So they are shown in inset maps.

An **inset map** is a small map within a larger map. An inset map may have its own scale. Map scales change depending on how much area is shown. Compare the map scales on the inset maps with the large map.

► One inch equals how many miles on the map of Hawaii?

► One inch equals how many miles on the map of Alaska?

► What can you tell about the sizes of Alaska and Hawaii?

► To figure the distance between Dallas and Houston, which map scale do you use?

► What is the distance between Dallas and Houston?

► Can you figure the distance between Honolulu and Los Angeles using these maps? Why or why not?

Figuring Distance in the United States

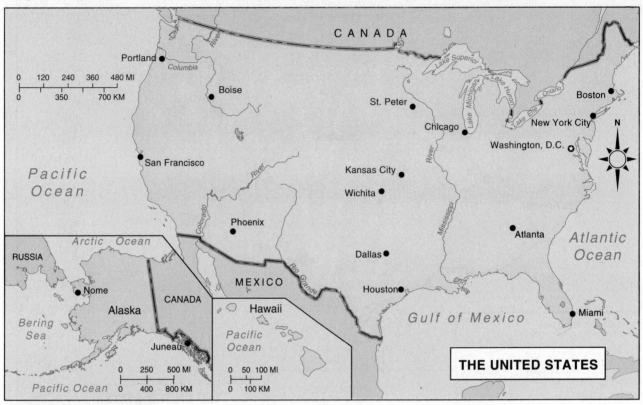

MAP ATTACK!

- **Read the title.** This map shows _____.
- **Read the map scale.** On the large map, one inch stands for
  _____ miles.

Use your ruler to figure these distances.

1. What two states are shown in the inset maps above? _____

   and _____

2. From Phoenix to Kansas City is about _____ miles.

3. From New York City to Washington, D.C. is about _____ miles.

4. From Kansas City to Boston is about _____ miles.

5. From Nome to Juneau is about _____ miles.

6. Is it farther from San Francisco to Houston or from Portland to Chicago?

   _____

Figuring Distance in the Great Lakes States

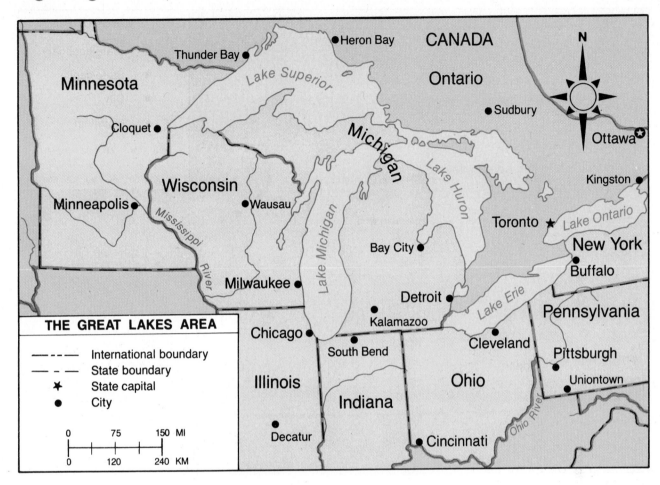

Use your ruler to figure these distances.

1. From Chicago to Decatur is about _____ miles.

2. From Wausau to Milwaukee is about _____ miles.

3. From Thunder Bay to Minneapolis is about _____ miles.

4. From Toronto to Buffalo is about _____ miles.

5. From Cleveland to Heron Bay is about _____ miles.

6. From Milwaukee to Ottawa is about _____ miles.

7. From Sudbury to Detroit is about _____ miles.

8. From Ottawa to Cincinnati is about _____ miles.

9. Is it farther from Chicago to Sudbury or from Heron Bay to Cleveland?

   _____

10. Is it farther from Ottawa to Kingston or from Milwaukee to Chicago?

    _____

Figuring Distance on a State Map

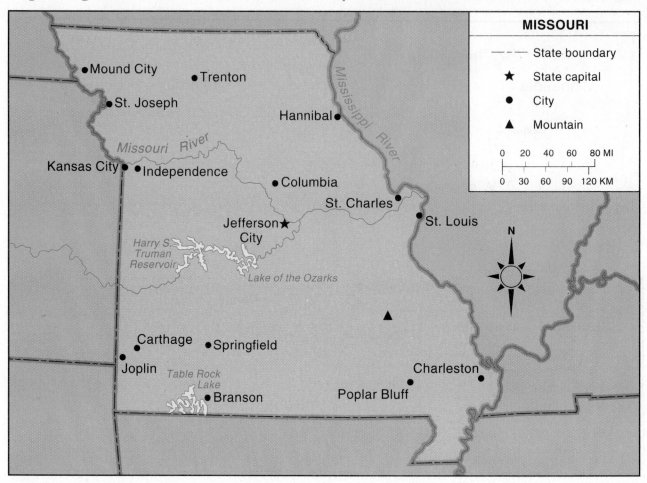

Imagine you are going on a tour of Missouri. Use a ruler to draw lines as you figure these distances and directions.

1. Find the state capital on the map. Circle it.

   a. What direction will you go from the state capital to Springfield?_____

   b. From the state capital to Springfield is about _____ miles.

2. a. What direction will you go from Springfield to Carthage? _____

   b. From Springfield to Carthage is about _____ miles.

3. a. What direction will you go from Carthage to Poplar Bluff? _____

   b. From Carthage to Poplar Bluff is about _____ miles.

4. a. What direction will you go from Poplar Bluff to St. Louis? _____

   b. From Poplar Bluff to St. Louis is about _____ miles.

5. There is a mountain about 80 miles southwest of St. Louis and about 60 miles northwest of Poplar Bluff. Find it on the map. Label it Taum Sauk Mountain. You have reached the highest point in Missouri!

Skill Check

Vocabulary Check   **map scale   miles   kilometers   inset map**

Use each word or phrase to finish a sentence.

1. A map scale shows distance in _____ and

   _____ .

2. A small map within a larger map is called an _____ .

3. A _____ is used to compare distance on a map with distance on Earth.

Map Check

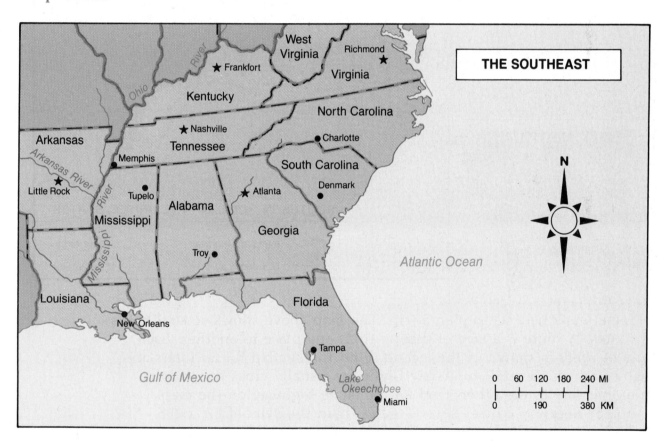

Use a ruler and the map scale to figure these distances.

1. From Atlanta to Richmond is about _____ miles.

2. From Memphis to Frankfort is about _____ miles.

3. From Nashville to Miami is about _____ miles.

4. Is it farther from Nashville to New Orleans or from Nashville to

   Richmond? _____

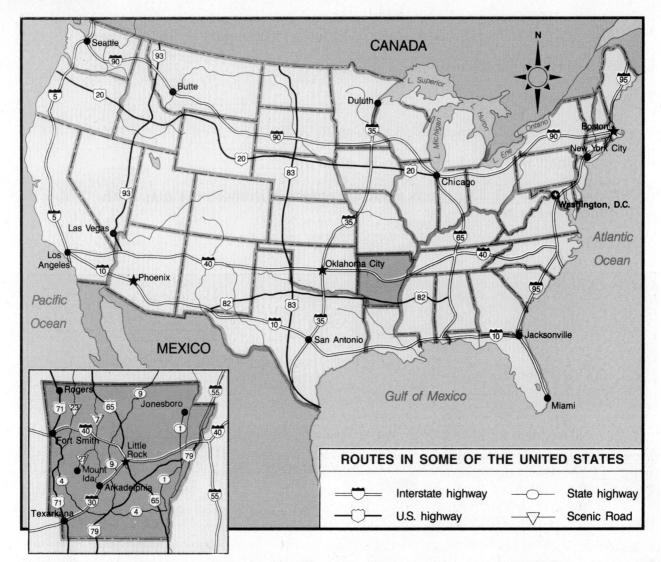

Some maps help us to plan a trip. The map above shows several kinds of routes. A **route** is a way of getting from one place to another. Each kind of route is shown in the legend. Find the symbol for an interstate highway in the legend. **Interstate highways** usually cross the country from one side to the other. Find an interstate highway on the map.

A **U.S. highway** crosses several states. Find the symbol for a U.S. highway in the legend. Then find a U.S. highway on the map.

State highways connect cities and towns within one state. **Scenic roads** cross areas that offer a beautiful view. Find the symbols for state highway and scenic road. Look at the inset map of Arkansas. What kinds of routes do you see?

► Interstate 35 connects what northern city with what southern city?

► U.S. 93 connects Las Vegas with the boundary of what country?

► What state highway crosses southern Arkansas?

► Where are the scenic roads in Arkansas?

► What U.S. highway passes through Little Rock?

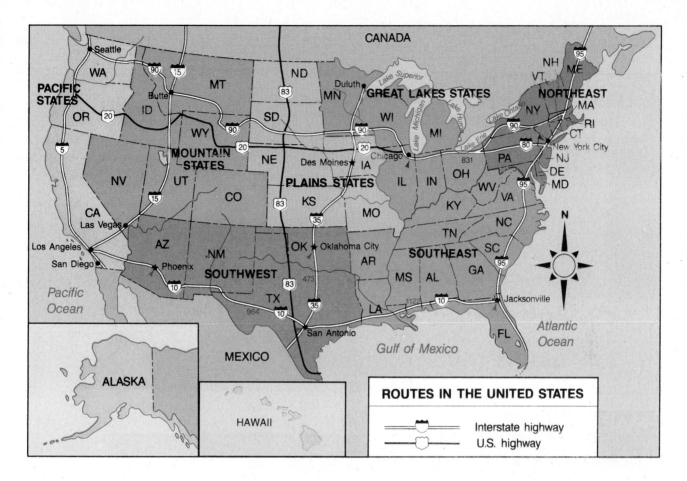

Look at the route map above. It shows interstate and U.S. highways crossing regions of the United States. A **region** is an area with many things in common. Find the Pacific States. Notice that all of the Pacific States touch the Pacific Ocean. What states are included in this region?

Three regions are named for intermediate directions. Find them. Name the states in the Southwest, the Southeast, and the Northeast.

Three regions are named for land or water forms. Find them. Name the states in the Mountain States, the Plains States, and the Great Lakes States.

Route maps often show the distance between cities. Find the small red triangle pointing to Chicago. That triangle is a **mileage marker**. The next mileage marker east of Chicago is in New York City. The distance from Chicago to New York City is 831 miles. Find the red number 831 near the route from Chicago to New York City.

► What lakes border the Great Lakes States?

► What regions does Interstate 10 cross?

► What regions does U.S. 83 cross?

► What interstate crosses the Mountain States from north to south?

► What U.S. highway crosses the Plains States from north to south?

► What highways would take you from Seattle to Las Vegas via (by way of) Butte?

► What is the distance from San Antonio to Jacksonville?

Reading a Route Map

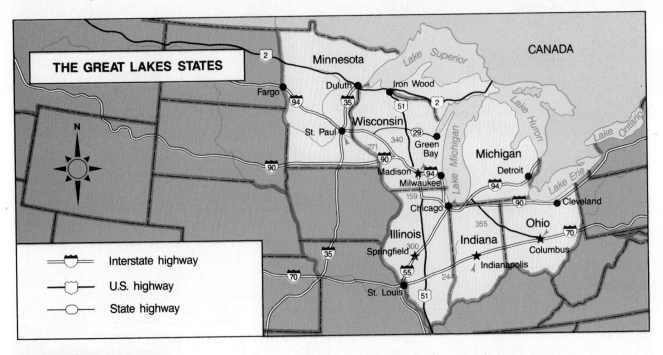

MAP ATTACK!

- **Read the title.** This map shows _____ .
- **Read the legend.** The three types of highways shown are _____,
  _____ , and _____ .
- **Read the compass rose.** Label the intermediate directions.

1. What states are included in this region? _____

   _____

2. Which of the Great Lakes border this region?

   _____

3. Trace the route from Green Bay to St. Paul. Use a green pencil or

   marker. What highways would you take? _____

4. Trace the route from Green Bay to Duluth via Iron Wood. Use a red

   pencil or marker. What highways would you take? _____

5. Is it farther from Chicago to St. Louis or from Chicago to Columbus?

   _____

6. Where would you see this sign?

Duluth	340
St. Paul	271
Chicago	159

_____

Reading a Route Map

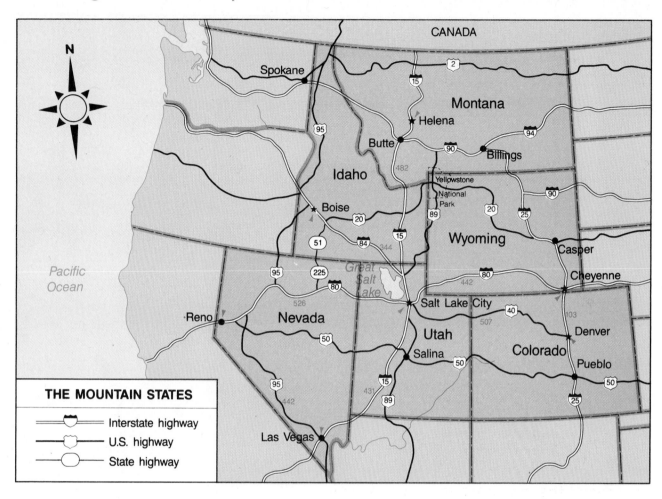

1. What region is shown here? _____

2. What states are in this region? _____

   _____

3. Trace the route from Helena to Salt Lake City in green.

   a. What highway takes you from Helena to Salt Lake City? _____

   b. How many miles is it from Helena to Salt Lake City? _____

   c. What states do you cross? _____

4. Trace the route from Helena to Cheyenne in orange. Be sure to go through Yellowstone National Park.

   What highways would you take? _____

5. What U.S. highway connects Interstate 84 with Interstate 80? _____

6. Where would you see this sign? _____
   (I stands for Interstate.)

Figuring Distance on a Route Map

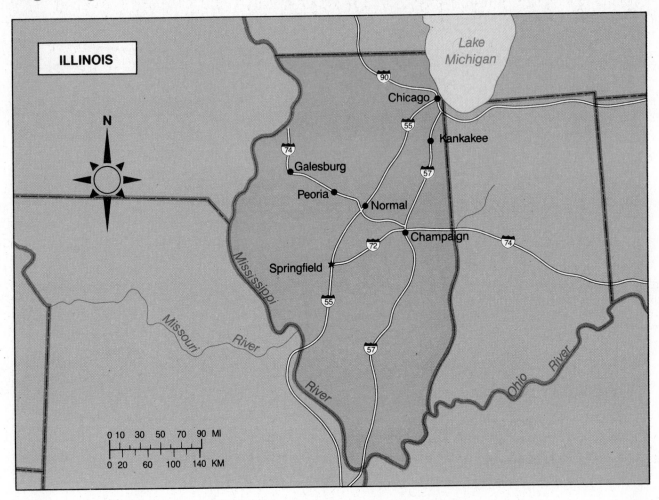

1. Circle the capital of Illinois on the map. Name it. _____
2. Chicago is the largest city in Illinois. Find it on the map and circle it.

3. From Chicago to Springfield is about _____ miles.
4. You want to find the shortest route from Chicago to Springfield. Would you drive Interstate 57 and Interstate 72 or Interstate 55 through

   Normal? _____

   What direction would you be traveling? _____

5. From Kankakee to Champaign is about _____ miles.

   What direction is Champaign from Kankakee? _____

6. From Springfield to Champaign is about _____ miles.

   What direction is Champaign from Springfield? _____

7. If you drove 40 miles an hour from Springfield to Champaign, how many

   hours would it take? _____

✓ Skill Check

Vocabulary Check

route   interstate highway   U.S. highway
state highway   scenic road   region
mileage marker

1. An _____ crosses the entire country.

2. A _____ crosses several states.

3. To figure distances on route maps, use the _____.

4. A _____ crosses one state.

5. An area with many things in common is a _____.

Map Check

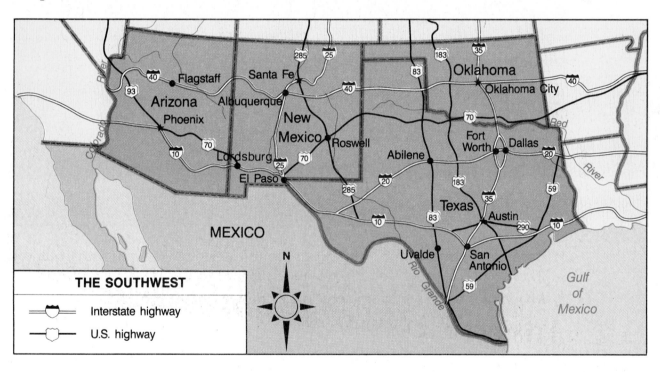

1. What interstate highway splits to go through Dallas and Fort Worth? ____

2. What route goes <u>through</u> the capital of Arizona? _____

3. What route goes along part of the Red River? _____

4. What route goes through both the capital of Oklahoma and the capital

   of Texas? _____

5. What interstate highways would you take from Flagstaff to Abilene via

   Albuquerque and El Paso? _____

 # Geography Themes Up Close

Movement describes how people, goods, information, and ideas move from place to place. Movement shows people interacting. It demonstrates **interdependence**, or how people depend on one another, to meet their needs and wants. The St. Lawrence Seaway is a waterway that connects the Atlantic Ocean with the Great Lakes. This waterway lies in Canada and in the United States.

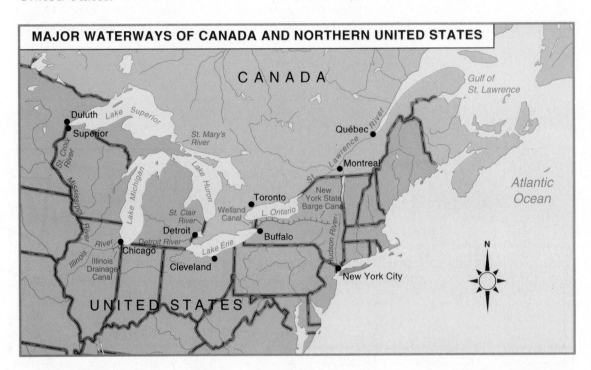

MAJOR WATERWAYS OF CANADA AND NORTHERN UNITED STATES

1. Trace the route of a ship that travels from the Atlantic Ocean into the Gulf of St. Lawrence, through the St. Lawrence Seaway, to the Mississippi River.

2. What major bodies of water does this ship pass through?

_____

_____

_____

3. What cities would the ship pass on its way to Chicago?

_____

4. What major bodies of water would a ship pass through, traveling from Duluth to New York City?

_____

_____

5. How do these waterways show interdependence and make the movement of people and goods easier between people in the United States and Canada?

_____

_____

_____

Charts show facts in columns and rows. The chart below shows facts about using communication tools.

Use of Communication Tools in the United States

Number of hours per person per year			
	1990	1995	2000 (est.)
Television	1,470	1,575	1,555
Radio	1,135	1,091	1,074
Newspapers	175	165	154
Books	95	99	98
Magazines	90	84	79
Internet	1	7	37

6. According to the chart, which communication tool is most used by people in

the United States? _____

7. Which communication tool is used the least in the United States? Why do you think this is so?

_____

_____

_____

Physical Maps

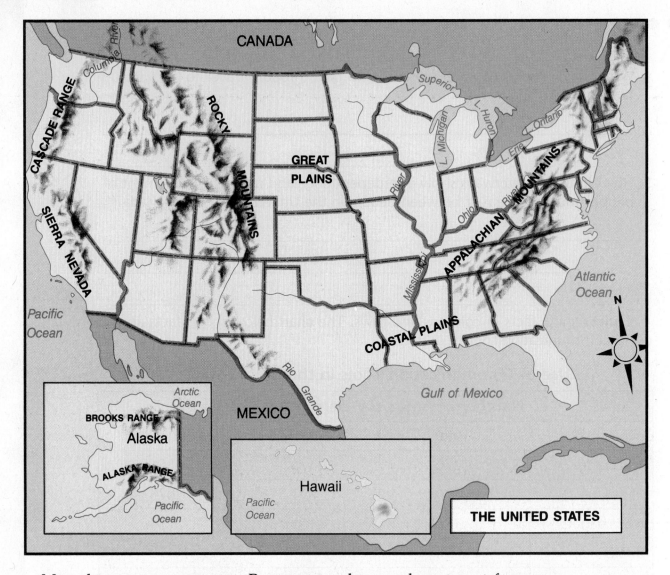

Maps have many purposes. Route maps show us how to get from one place to another. **Relief maps** show different landforms on Earth. Look at the relief map above. It shows the United States. You can see mountain ranges, plains, lakes, and rivers.

A **mountain range** is a group or chain of mountains. Find the Rocky Mountains on the map. A **plain** is a large area of level, treeless land. Now find the Great Plains. Which is darker, the mountains or the plains?

Relief maps help us picture how the land looks. The dark shading on relief maps stands for mountains. Higher mountains appear the darkest. Since plains are very flat, we do not see any shading.

► Locate your own state. Is your state mostly mountains or plains?

► Name the mountain ranges and plains shown on the map.

► What is the highest mountain range on the map? How do you know?

► Are there more mountains in the eastern or in the western United States?

► Locate the inset map of Alaska. Are there more mountains or plains?

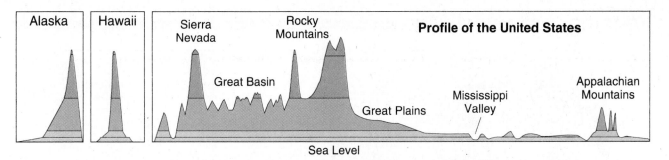

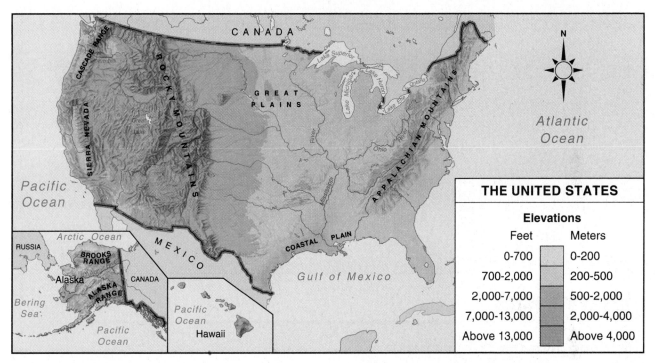

Sea level is the level of the ocean surface. Land that is even with the ocean is at sea level. Land that is higher than the ocean is above sea level. **Elevation** means the height of the land above sea level. Look at the diagram. It shows a side-view of the mountains, valleys, and plains of the United States. Each color in the legend and diagram stands for a different elevation. Elevation is measured in feet or meters.

A **physical map** combines elevation and relief. The physical maps above show the United States. The colors in the legend tell you the elevation of the land. This makes it easy to understand what the United States really looks like. Physical maps may also show cities, boundaries, mountain peaks, and rivers.

► On the map above, what color shows the elevation of the highest mountain peaks?

► What color is used to show the elevation of the Great Plains?

► Locate the area on the map where you live.
What is the elevation of the area where you live?

► Find the Rocky Mountains in the diagram. What colors are used to show their elevation? Find the Rocky Mountains on the map. What colors are used to show their elevation?

Reading a Physical Map

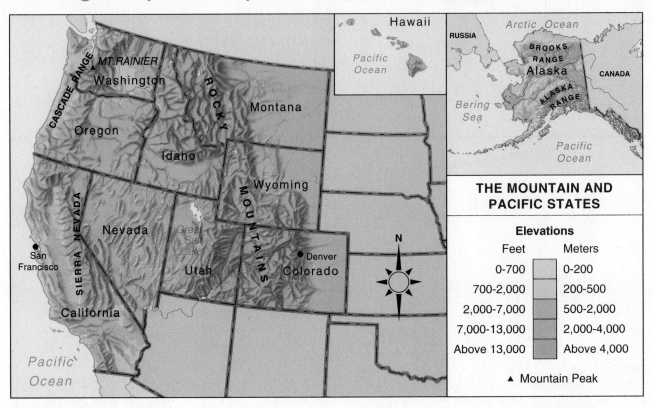

THE MOUNTAIN AND PACIFIC STATES

Elevations

Feet		Meters
0-700		0-200
700-2,000		200-500
2,000-7,000		500-2,000
7,000-13,000		2,000-4,000
Above 13,000		Above 4,000

▲ Mountain Peak

MAP ATTACK!

- **Read the title.** This map shows _____.

- **Read the legend.** What color is land above 13,000 feet? _____
- **Read the compass rose.** Circle the intermediate direction arrows.

1. Which color in the legend stands for the lowest elevation? _____

Complete each sentence below.

2. Find the Great Salt Lake in Utah. The elevation of this area is between

    2,000 and 7,000 feet or between _____ and _____ meters.

3. Find Denver, Colorado. The elevation of this city is between _____

    and _____ feet or between _____ and _____ meters.

4. Find San Francisco, California. The elevation of this city is

    between _____ and _____ feet or between _____ and

    _____ meters.

5. Find the symbol for mountain peak in the legend. What is the name of a

    mountain peak in the state of Washington? _____

Reading a Physical Map

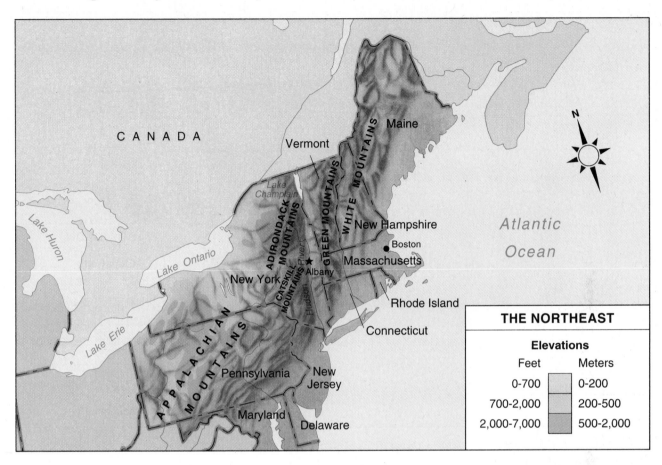

1. Look at the land along the coast of the Atlantic Ocean. Is this land

   mountainous or flat?_____

2. Which state has only low elevation and is all the same color?

   _____

3. Which are higher, the Catskill Mountains or the White Mountains?

   _____

4. What lake lies near the northwestern edge of the Green Mountains?

   _____

5. Trace the Hudson River. The Hudson River flows into what body of

   water?_____

6. The elevation of Boston is between _____ and _____ feet or

   between _____ and _____ meters.

7. Draw a conclusion. Would it be easy to hike from the White Mountains

   to Albany? Why or why not?_____

Reading a Physical Map

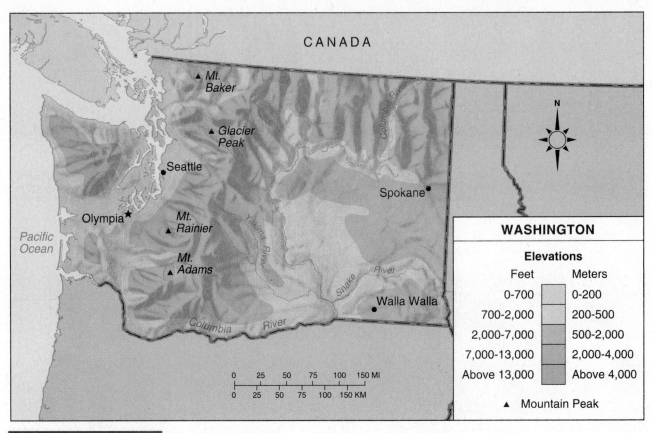

MAP ATTACK!

Follow the steps on page 38 to begin reading this map.

1. What is the state capital of Washington?_____

2. The elevation of the state capital is between _____ and _____ feet.

3. What direction is Seattle from the state capital? _____

4. How many miles is it from the state capital to Seattle? Use a ruler and the map scale. The distance is about _____ miles.

5. From Seattle, which direction would you travel to reach an international border? _____

6. From Seattle, which direction would you travel to reach a boundary formed by a river? _____

7. Which is higher, Seattle or Spokane? _____

8. Draw a conclusion. Draw a line from Walla Walla to Seattle. What problems would you face if you built a highway from Walla Walla to Seattle? _____

✓ Skill Check

Vocabulary Check
     relief map   **plain**   **mountain range**
     physical map **elevation**

1. The height of the land in feet or meters is called _____.

2. A _____ is a group of mountains.

3. A _____ shows the landforms on Earth.

4. A _____ is a large area of flat land.

5. A map that shows changes in elevation is called a _____.

Map Check

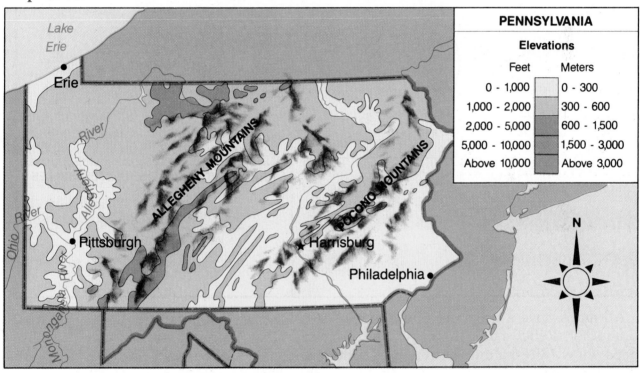

1. Which mountains are higher, the Allegheny Mountains or the Pocono

  Mountains? _____

2. What three rivers meet in Pittsburgh?

  _____

3. Is Erie at a higher or lower elevation than Philadelphia? _____

4. What is the state capital of Pennsylvania? _____

5. The elevation of the state capital is between _____ and _____

  feet or between _____ and _____ meters.

6  Special Purpose Maps

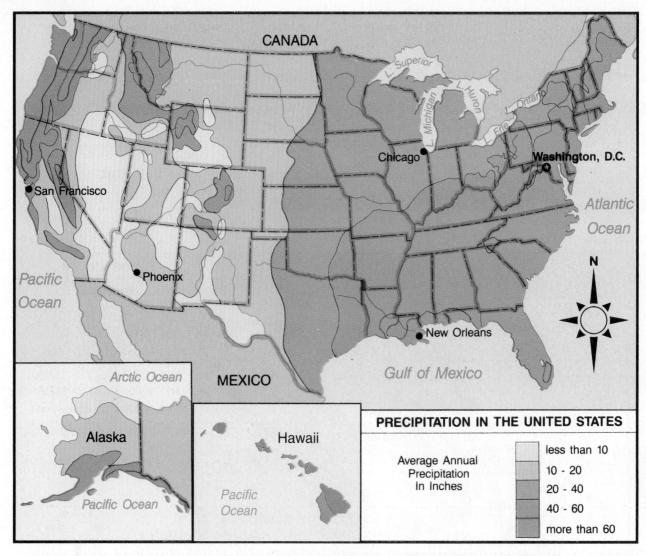

CANADA

L. Superior

L. Michigan

L. Huron

L. Ontario

Erie

Chicago

Washington, D.C.

San Francisco

Atlantic
Ocean

Pacific
Ocean

Phoenix

N

New Orleans

MEXICO

Gulf of Mexico

Arctic Ocean

Alaska

Hawaii

Pacific Ocean

Pacific
Ocean

PRECIPITATION IN THE UNITED STATES

Average Annual
Precipitation
In Inches

less than 10

10 - 20

20 - 40

40 - 60

more than 60

All maps have a purpose. Route maps show ways to get from one place
to another. Relief maps show us how the land looks. **Special purpose**
maps show information not found on other maps. The information may
be about the climate, the people, the resources, or the history of an area.
You need to read each map's title and legend carefully.

Use the map reading skills you've learned to read a special purpose map.
Read the title carefully. The title tells you what the map shows. This map
shows precipitation in the United States. Precipitation is rain and snow.

Read the legend carefully. The legend tells you what the symbols
mean. On this map, colors are used as symbols. Remember that a **symbol**
is something that stands for something else. Here each color stands for a
different amount of precipitation.

► What color stands for 20-40 inches of precipitation per year?
What areas on the map get 20-40 inches of precipitation per year?

► Does more precipitation fall along the coastlines or inland?

► Which area of the United States gets the most precipitation?

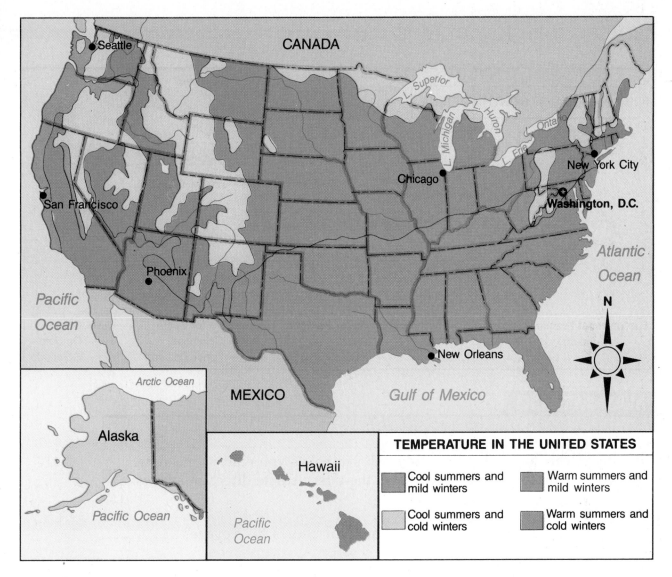

There are many types of special purpose maps. A **resource map** uses symbols for things in nature that people can use. In the legend you may find symbols for things like gold, oil, or coal. These symbols will appear on the map in the area where the resource is found.

Population maps show the number of people living in an area. The population of an area may be shown by using colors, dots of different sizes, or both.

Above is a **temperature map**. The legend shows summer and winter temperatures in the United States. It tells you that green areas have warm summers and cold winters. What color shows warm summers and mild winters?

► What kind of temperatures does New York City have?

► Look at the inset maps. What kind of temperatures do Alaska and Hawaii have?

► What kind of temperatures does Seattle have?

► Locate your state on the map on page 42 and the map above. Describe the climate where you live. What kind ot temperatures and how much precipitation does your state have?

Reading a Historical Map

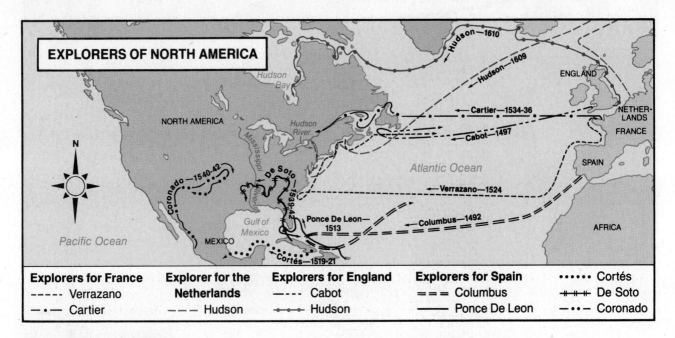

EXPLORERS OF NORTH AMERICA

Explorers for France	Explorer for the Netherlands	Explorers for England	Explorers for Spain	
----- Verrazano	----- Hudson	---- Cabot	=== Columbus	····· Cortés
—·— Cartier	— — Hudson	·—·—·— Hudson	—— Ponce De Leon	—+—+— De Soto
				—··— Coronado

MAP ATTACK!

- **Read the title.** This map shows _____.
- **Read the legend.** Check (✔) each symbol as you read its meaning.
- **Read the compass rose.** Label the intermediate direction arrows.

1. Find Columbus in the legend. What color shows his voyage? _____

2. In what country did Columbus start? _____

3. Which explorer made two trips to the New World? _____

   a. Where did he begin his first voyage? _____

   b. In what years were his voyages? _____
   c. What is a body of water named after this explorer?

   _____

4. Trace DeSoto's route in red.

   What river did he cross? _____

5. Trace Coronado's route in blue.

   In what country did he start? _____

6. DeSoto and Coronado were explorers for what country? _____

7. Draw a conclusion. Did most of the explorers for Spain travel to the

   northern or southern regions of North America? _____

Reading a Population Map

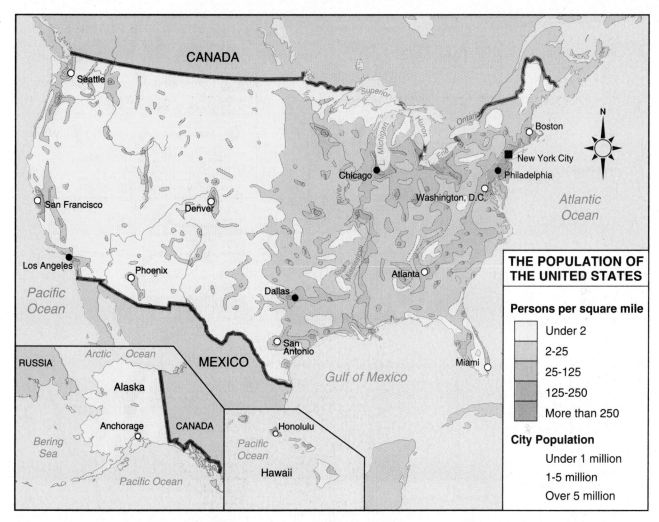

THE POPULATION OF THE UNITED STATES

Persons per square mile
- Under 2
- 2-25
- 25-125
- 125-250
- More than 250

City Population
- Under 1 million
- 1-5 million
- Over 5 million

1. The purpose of this map is to show

   _____.

2. What color shows less than 10 people per square mile? _____
3. Do you find more of this color in the eastern or in the western United

   States? _____

4. What color shows more than 500 people per square mile? _____
5. Add these symbols to the legend.   ○ City of under 1 million

                                       ● 1–5 million

                                       ■ Over 5 million

6. Name three cities that have 1 to 5 million people _____

   _____ and _____

7. What city has the largest population? _____

Reading a Land Use Map

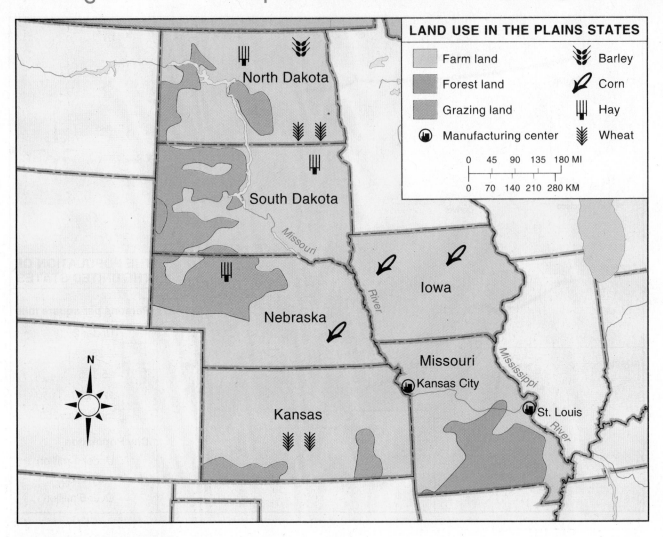

LAND USE IN THE PLAINS STATES

- Farm land
- Forest land
- Grazing land
- Manufacturing center
- Barley
- Corn
- Hay
- Wheat

0 45 90 135 180 MI

0 70 140 210 280 KM

North Dakota

South Dakota

Missouri

Nebraska

Iowa

Missouri

Kansas City

St. Louis

Mississippi River

Kansas

N

MAP ATTACK!

Follow the steps on page 44 to begin reading this map.

1. The purpose of this map is to show _____ .

2. What is the most common use of land in these states? _____

3. In which state is barley grown? _____

4. In which states is corn grown? _____

5. What is the most common use of land in western South Dakota?

   _____

6. In what part of Kansas is there grazing land? _____

7. There are two manufacturing centers in this region. Circle them.

   a. What are they? _____

   b. About how far apart are they? _____

Skill Check

Vocabulary Check   **special purpose map   temperature map   symbol**
    resource map   population map

Write the word that makes each sentence true.

1. A map showing the number of people in an area is a _____.

2. A map showing special information is a _____.

3. A _____ shows things found in nature that people can use.

Map Check

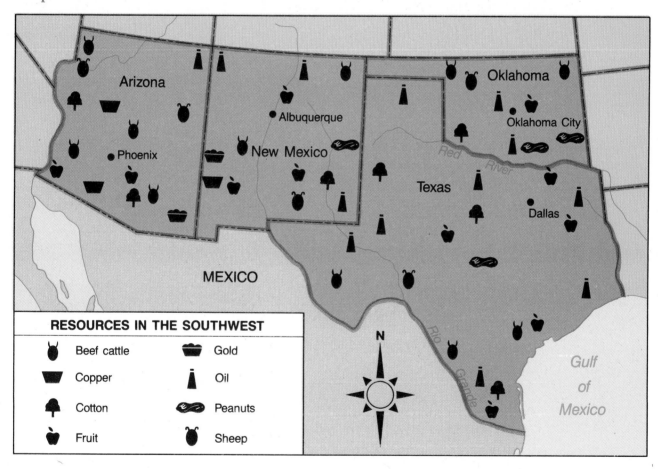

1. Gold is found in which states? _____

2. Is there more oil in Arizona or in Texas? _____

3. Cotton can be found in every state on this map. Name two other

   resources that can be found in all four states. _____

4. Which state does not grow peanuts? _____

5. Copper is found in which two states? _____

Geography Themes Up Close

Human/Environment Interaction shows how the environment and people affect one another. Sometimes people create problems. An example is pollution. One kind of pollution is **acid rain**—pollution that mixes with water vapor and falls to the ground in the form of rain or snow. This pollution comes from factories, power plants, and cars and trucks that burn coal, oil, and gas. Acid rain kills fish and destroys forests. It pollutes drinking water and soil and damages buildings. The map below shows recent acid rain levels in the United States and Canada.

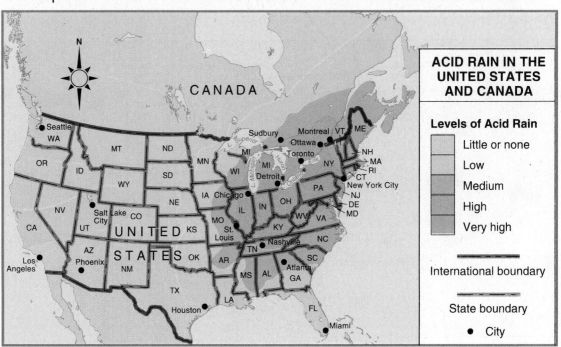

1. According to the map, where are the highest levels of acid rain found?

_____

_____

_____

2. Describe acid rain levels in western Canada and the western United States.

_____

_____

3. Based on the map, where do you think most manufacturing centers are located in the United States and Canada? Explain your answer.

_____

_____

_____

Human/Environment Interaction includes how people depend on the environment. The map shown here demonstrates how people in Mexico use the land and its resources to meet their needs and wants.

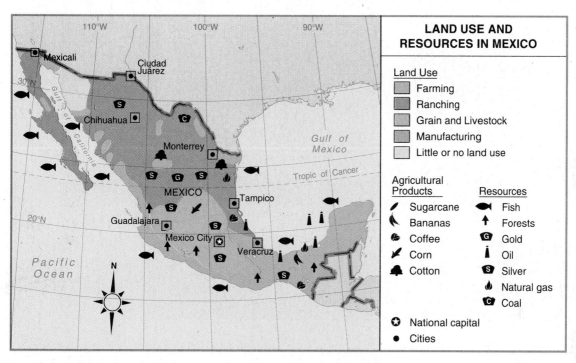

4. According to the map, where is fishing an important activity?

_____

5. Where is manufacturing an important activity?

_____

6. Where is most of the farming done in Mexico?

_____

7. Based on the map key and map, where would you expect Mexico's population to be the smallest?

_____

8. Along which of these coasts would be a better location for oil refineries: Pacific Ocean, Gulf of Mexico, or Gulf of California? Why?

_____

_____

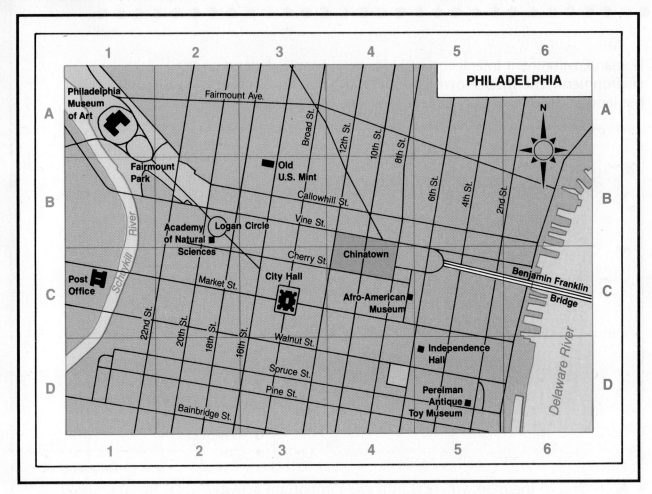

A **grid** is a pattern of lines drawn on a map to help people locate places. These lines form squares. Do you see the squares on the map above?

Now find the letters at each side of the map. The letters label the rows of squares. Numbers at the top and bottom label the columns of squares.

Locate City Hall on the map above. It is in square C-3. Find the letter C on the left side of the map. Slide your finger across row C until you reach column 3. You are now in square C-3. Put your finger on City Hall.

► Now move your finger one square to the east.
This is square C-4. Name two points of interest in C-4.

► Find the Perelman Antique Toy Museum. It is in square D-5.
Name another historic site in this square that you could visit.

► The Philadelphia Museum of Art is in square A-1.
This museum is in what park?
Put your finger on the museum. Slide it southeast through the park.
The park ends near Logan Circle. In what grid square is Logan Circle?

► Locate the Benjamin Franklin Bridge in square C-6.
What river does it cross?
Can you name the other grid squares that this river flows through?

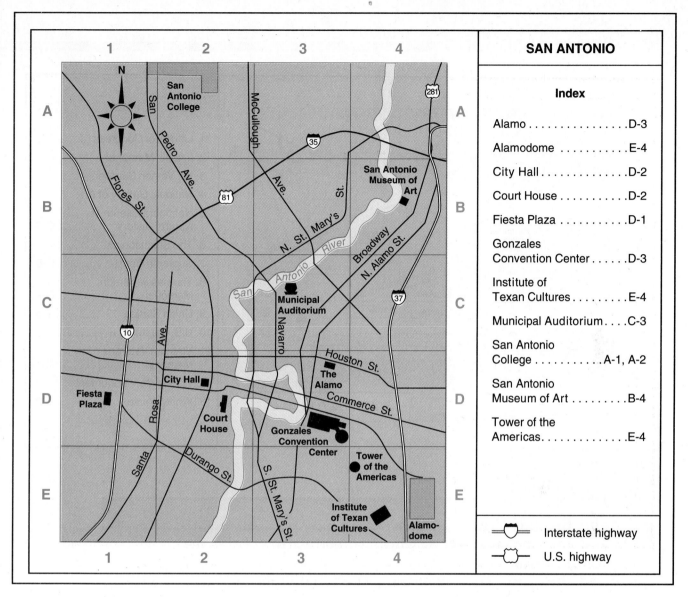

SAN ANTONIO

Index

Alamo D-3

Alamodome E-4

City Hall D-2

Court House D-2

Fiesta Plaza D-1

Gonzales
Convention Center D-3

Institute of
Texan Cultures E-4

Municipal Auditorium C-3

San Antonio
College A-1, A-2

San Antonio
Museum of Art B-4

Tower of the
Americas E-4

⬡ Interstate highway

⬡ U.S. highway

To find a place on a map grid, you can look it up in the map index. A **map index** is an alphabetical list of all the places shown on the map. A map index lists each place with the letter and number of its grid square.

Look at the map above. It shows places of interest in San Antonio, Texas. To find places on the map, you use the map index. Imagine you want to visit the Alamo. Look up "Alamo" in the map index. It directs you to square D-3. Locate square D-3 on the grid. Do you see the Alamo?

▶ Use the map index to find City Hall. In what grid square is it located?
  Find City Hall on the map. Name another point of interest in this square.

▶ Look up the San Antonio Museum of Art in the map index.
  In what grid square is it located?
  What direction is the San Antonio Museum of Art from City Hall?

▶ Find San Antonio College by using the map index.
  In what grid squares is it located?

▶ Locate the Institute of Texan Cultures using the map index.
  In what grid square is it located?
  What other points of interest are located in this same square?

Reading a Map Grid

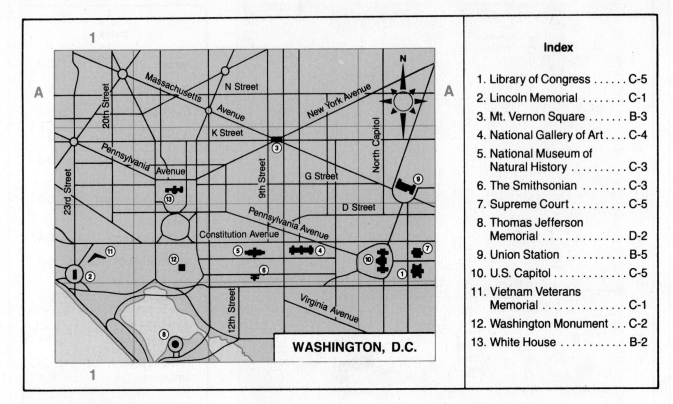

Index

1. Library of Congress C-5
2. Lincoln Memorial C-1
3. Mt. Vernon Square B-3
4. National Gallery of Art C-4
5. National Museum of
   Natural History C-3
6. The Smithsonian C-3
7. Supreme Court C-5
8. Thomas Jefferson
   Memorial D-2
9. Union Station B-5
10. U.S. Capitol C-5
11. Vietnam Veterans
    Memorial C-1
12. Washington Monument . . . C-2
13. White House B-2

WASHINGTON, D.C.

MAP ATTACK!

- **Read the title.** This map shows _____.
- **Read the compass rose.** Circle the north arrow. Label the intermediate directions.
- **Read the grid.** Add the missing letters and numbers.

Use the index and map to answer these questions.

1. In what square is the White House located? _____
   Circle it on the map.

2. In what square is the Washington Monument? _____
   Circle it on the map.
   What famous memorial is south of the Washington Monument?

   _____

   What memorial is to the northwest? _____

3. In what square is the U.S. Capitol located? _____

   What two points of interest are to the east? _____

   _____

Reading a Map Grid

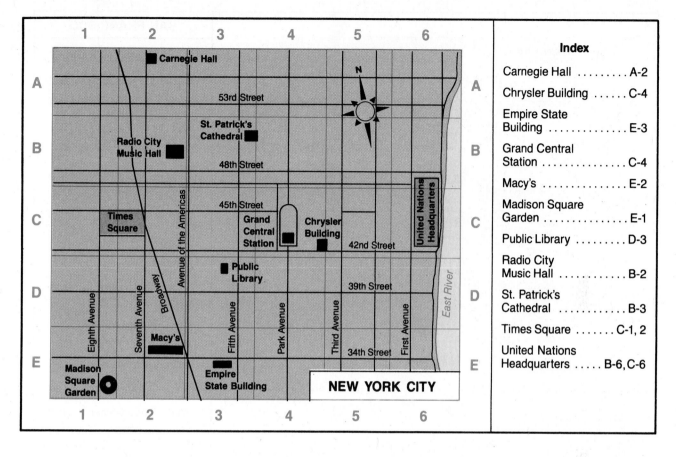

1. In what squares is the United Nations Headquarters located? _____
   What avenue goes along the west side of the United Nations

   Headquarters? _____

2. In what grid squares is Times Square located? _____
   Draw a line along 42nd Street from the United Nations Headquarters
   to Times Square.

   Name one building you pass. _____

3. In what grid square is Radio City Music Hall located? _____
   Trace your route from Times Square to Radio City Music Hall.
   What avenue is just east of Radio City Music Hall?

   _____

4. In what grid square is the Empire State Building? _____
   Trace your route from Radio City Music Hall east to Fifth Avenue.
   Trace your route to the Empire State Building.
   What street is just north of the Empire State Building?

   _____

Reading a Map Grid

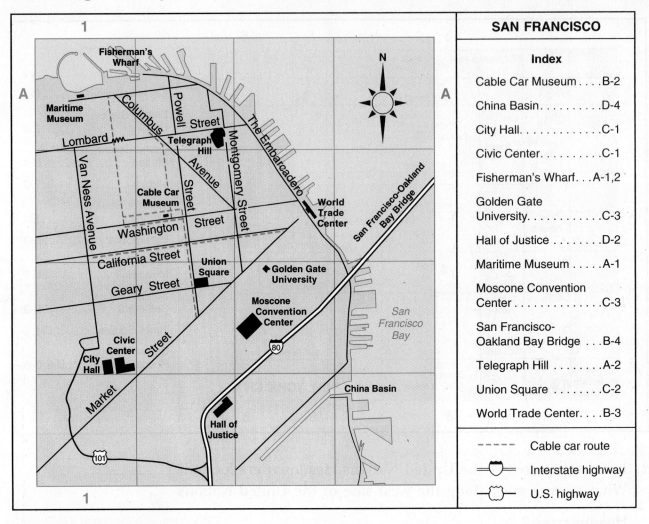

SAN FRANCISCO

Index

Cable Car Museum B-2

China Basin. D-4

City Hall. C-1

Civic Center. C-1

Fisherman's Wharf. . . A-1,2

Golden Gate
University. C-3

Hall of Justice D-2

Maritime Museum A-1

Moscone Convention
Center C-3

San Francisco-
Oakland Bay Bridge . . . B-4

Telegraph Hill A-2

Union Square C-2

World Trade Center. . . . B-3

- - - - - Cable car route

Interstate highway

U.S. highway

MAP ATTACK!

Follow the steps on page 52 to begin reading this map.

1. In what grid square do you find the Maritime Museum? _____
   Circle it on the map.

2. In what grid square is the Cable Car Museum located? _____
   Circle it on the map.

3. What direction is the Maritime Museum from the Cable Car Museum?

   _____

4. Trace the cable car route from the Cable Car Museum to Union Square.

   Is Union Square east or west of the cable car route? _____

5. What interstate highway is in San Francisco? _____

6. What U.S. highway is in San Francisco? _____

✓ Skill Check

Vocabulary Check   **grid**   **map index**

1. A pattern of lines drawn on a map is called a _____.

2. A _____ is an alphabetized list of all the places shown on a map.

Map Check

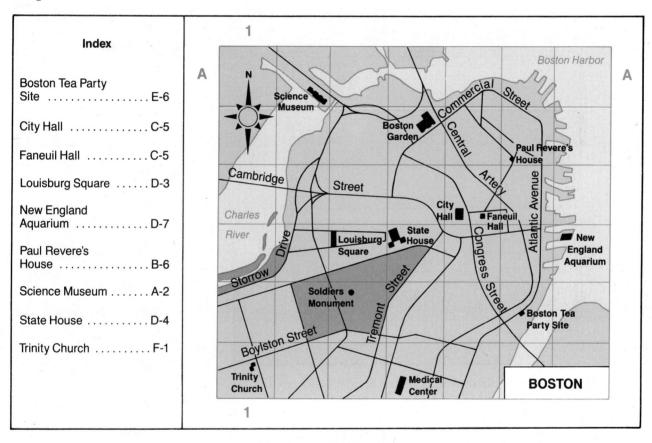

1. Complete the grid by adding the missing letters and numbers.

2. In what grid square do you find City Hall? _____
    Circle it.

3. In what grid square do you find Paul Revere's House? _____

    What direction is Paul Revere's House from City Hall? _____ .

4. In what grid square is the New England Aquarium located? _____

    What direction is the Aquarium from Paul Revere's House? _____

5. In what grid square is the Boston Tea Party Site located? _____

    What direction is it from City Hall? _____

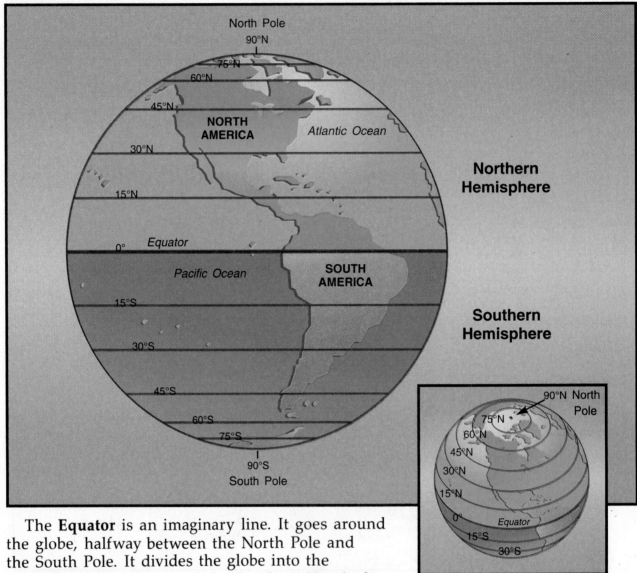

The **Equator** is an imaginary line. It goes around the globe, halfway between the North Pole and the South Pole. It divides the globe into the **Northern Hemisphere** and the **Southern Hemisphere**. Remember that the globe is a sphere. A **hemisphere** is half of a sphere.

The Equator is the most important line of **latitude**. The other lines of latitude measure distance on a globe north or south of the Equator. We use lines of latitude to locate places on the globe.

► Find the Equator on the large globe above.
  It is marked 0°. The symbol ° stands for **degrees**.

► Find the 45°N line of latitude. What continent does it cross?

► Find the 45°S line of latitude. What continent does it cross?

Lines of latitude are also called **parallels**. Lines of latitude never touch.

► Look at the small globe above.
  Find the 75°N parallel.
  Does it touch any other parallel?
  What continents does it cross?

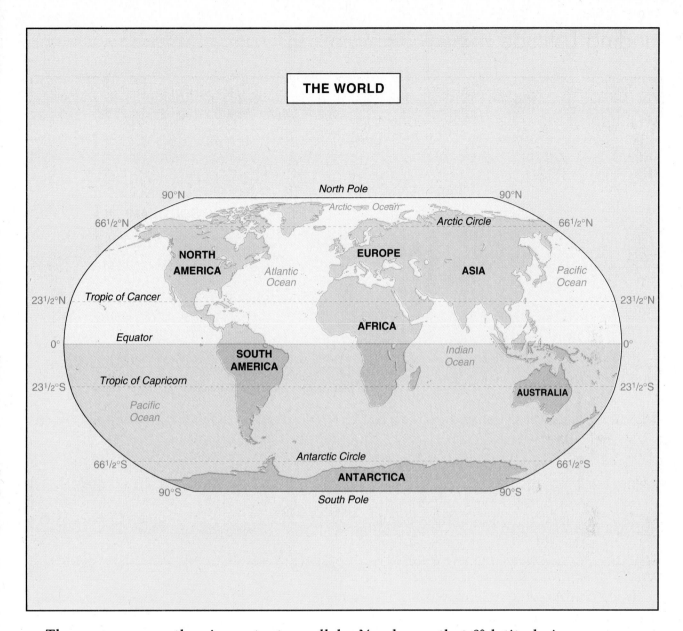

THE WORLD

There are some other important parallels. You know that 0° latitude is called the Equator. Other lines of latitude also have names. Find the line south of the Equator marked 23½°S. That line is called the **Tropic of Capricorn**.

Find the line north of the Equator marked 23½°N. That line is called the **Tropic of Cancer**.

Two other important lines of latitude are the **Arctic Circle** and the **Antarctic Circle**. The Arctic Circle is 66½°N of the Equator. Find the Arctic Circle on the map above. The Antarctic Circle is 66½°S of the Equator. Find the Antarctic Circle on the map above.

► The Tropic of Cancer goes through which continents?

► The Tropic of Capricorn goes through which oceans?

► The Arctic Circle goes through which continents?

► The Antarctic Circle goes around which continent?

► Which important parallel do you live nearest?

Finding Latitude

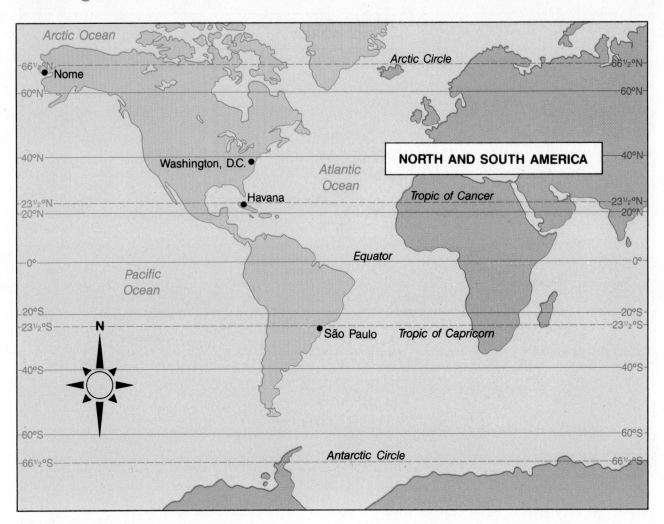

1. Trace the Arctic Circle in red.

   The Arctic Circle is in which hemisphere? _____

   What city lies near the Arctic Circle? _____

2. Trace the Antarctic Circle in blue.

   The Antarctic Circle is in which hemisphere? _____

   What oceans does the Antarctic Circle touch? _____

3. Trace the Tropic of Cancer in orange.

   The Tropic of Cancer is in which hemisphere? _____

   What city lies near the Tropic of Cancer? _____

4. Trace the Tropic of Capricorn in green. The Tropic of Capricorn

   is in which hemisphere? _____

   What city lies near the Tropic of Capricorn? _____

Finding Latitude

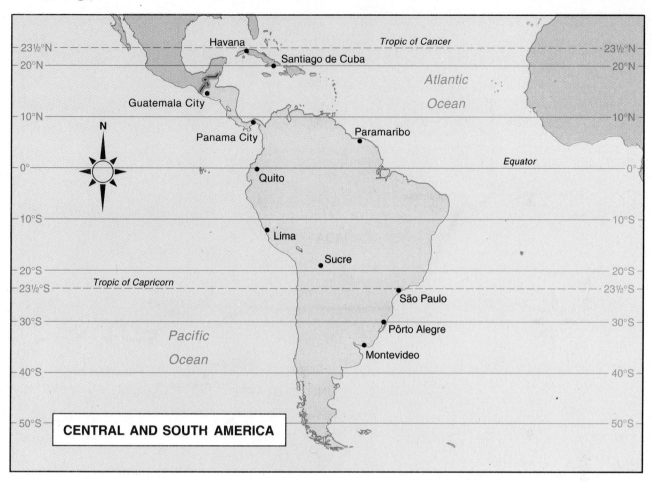

CENTRAL AND SOUTH AMERICA

1. What city lies on the Equator? _____

2. What city lies near the Tropic of Cancer? _____

3. What city lies near the Tropic of Capricorn? _____

4. What city lies near 20°N? _____

5. What city lies near 10°N? _____

6. What city lies near 20°S? _____

7. What city lies at 30°S? _____

8. Guatemala City lies between 20°N and 10°N.

   Estimate its latitude. _____

9. Paramaribo lies between 10°N and the Equator.

   Estimate its latitude. _____

10. Montevideo lies between 30°S and 40°S.

    Estimate its latitude. _____

Finding Latitude

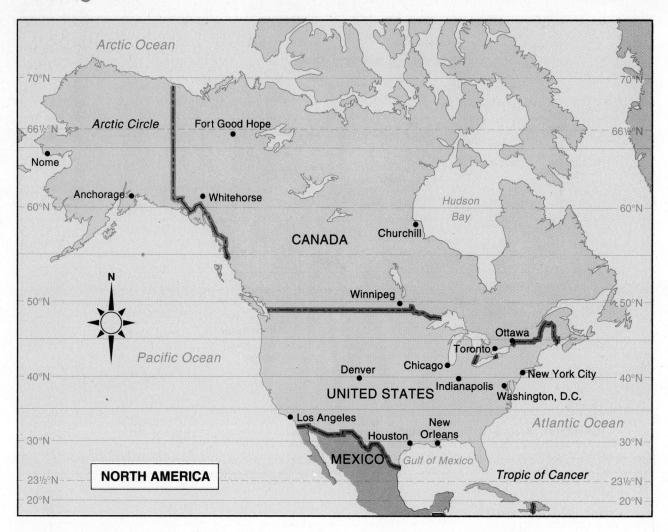

1. What two cities lie at 30°N? _____

2. What two cities lie at 40°N? _____

3. What city lies at 50°N? _____

4. What is another name for 66½°N latitude? _____

5. What city lies near the Arctic Circle? _____

6. Find Ottawa. It lies between 40°N and 50°N.

   Estimate its latitude. _____

7. Find Los Angeles. It lies between 30°N and 40°N.

   Estimate its latitude. _____

8. What border runs along the 49°N line of latitude?

   _____

9. Is Canada north or south of the Tropic of Cancer? _____

Skill Check

Vocabulary Check

Equator	latitude	parallel
Tropic of Capricorn	Tropic of Cancer	degrees
Arctic Circle	Antarctic Circle	
Northern Hemisphere	Southern Hemisphere	

1. Another name for a line of latitude is a _____.

2. Latitude is measured in _____.

Map Check

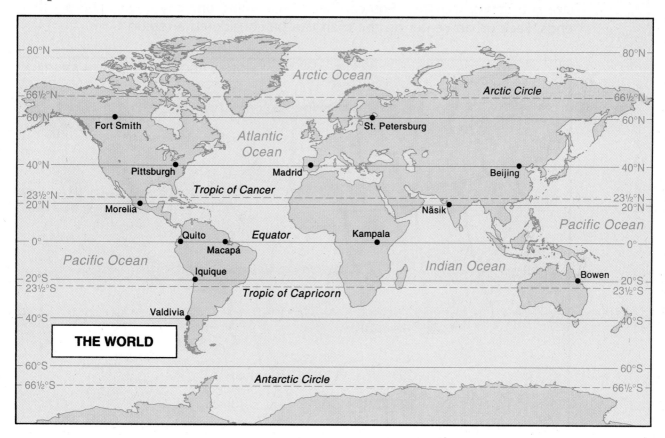

1. Label the Northern Hemisphere and the Southern Hemisphere on the map above.

2. What is another name for 66½°S latitude? _____

3. What is another name for 23½°N latitude? _____

4. What two cities lie at 60°N? _____

5. What two cities lie at 20°S? _____

6. What two cities lie at 20°N? _____

7. What is the latitude of Quito? _____

Geography Themes Up Close

Regions describes places that share one or more features. A region can be called physical because it is marked by a physical feature, such as climate. The Great Plains is a physical region of the United States that has grasslands as its common feature. A region can be called a human region if it is marked by a human feature, such as language.

The map shows the major urban centers in the United States and Canada. Each center is made up of several large cities and their suburbs that have increased in size and grown together. You can hardly tell where one city begins and another ends. Each urban center on the map can be considered a region.

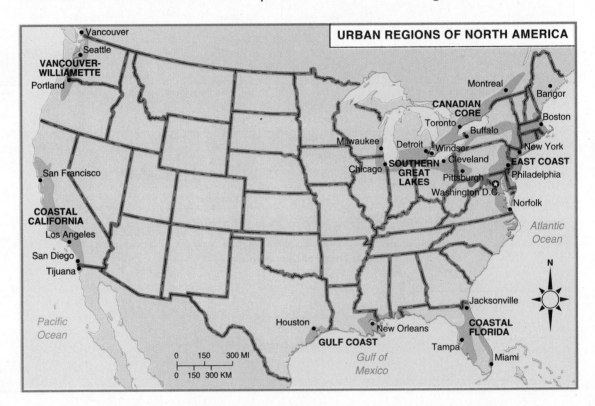

1. What is similar about the location of each urban region in North America?

_____

2. Use a ruler and the map scale. How many miles long is the Coastal California urban region?

_____

3. What cities make up the Vancouver-Willamette urban region?

_____

Regions can be as large as a hemisphere or as small as a neighborhood. The map shows neighborhoods in New Orleans that can be considered regions.

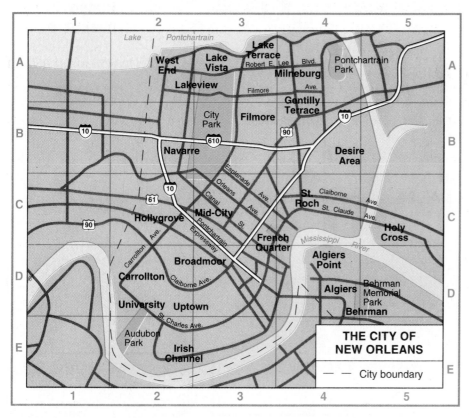

4. The Garden District is found in grid square D-3. This region has many old mansions and beautiful gardens. Label Garden District on the map.

5. What feature do you think the neighborhood called Lakeview has in common?

_____

6. What special features would you expect to find in the French Quarter?

_____

_____

7. How could these neighborhood regions help the government of New Orleans organize the city?

_____

_____

_____

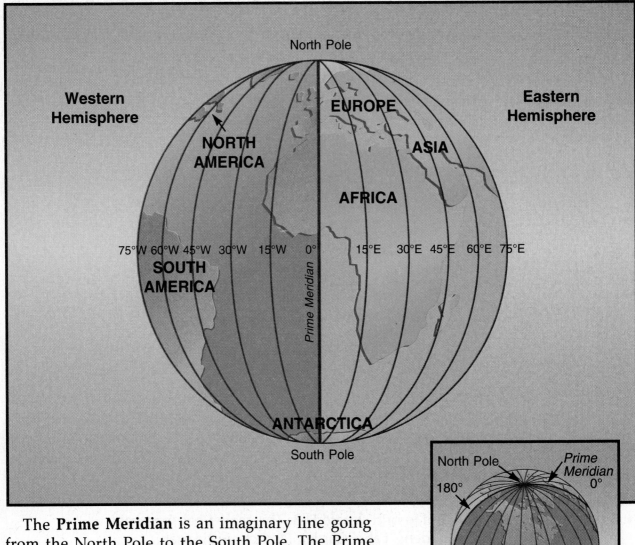

The **Prime Meridian** is an imaginary line going from the North Pole to the South Pole. The Prime Meridian is a line of **longitude**. It is marked 0°. The other lines of longitude measure distance on a globe east and west of the Prime Meridian. All lines of longitude meet at the North and South Poles. Lines of longitude are also called **meridians**.

The 180° meridian and the Prime Meridian form a circle around the globe. That circle divides the globe into two hemispheres. The hemisphere east of the Prime Meridian is the **Eastern Hemisphere**. The hemisphere west of the Prime Meridian is the **Western Hemisphere**.

► Find the Prime Meridian on the large globe above. What continents does it cross?

► What continents and oceans are in the Eastern Hemisphere?

► What continents and oceans are in the Western Hemisphere?

► Find the 45°West meridian. What continents does it cross?

► Find the 45°East meridian. What continents does it cross?

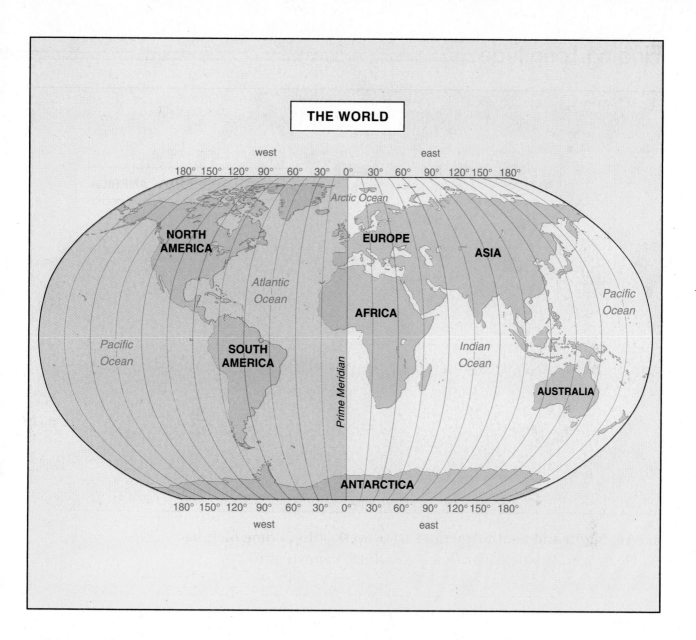

THE WORLD

Lines of longitude are measured in degrees. The Prime Meridian is 0°. All other meridians are numbered east and west of the Prime Meridian up to 180°. The meridians in the Eastern Hemisphere are marked with an *E*. The meridians in the Western Hemisphere are marked with a *W*.

► Find the Prime Meridian on the map.
  What oceans does it cross?

► Find the 180° meridian on each side of the map.
  Even though you see it twice, it is really the same line.
  What oceans does the 180° meridian cross?

► Find the 30°E meridian.
  What continents does the 30°E meridian cross?

► Find the 60°W meridian.
  What continents does the 60°W meridian cross?

► Why do the meridians curve?

Finding Longitude

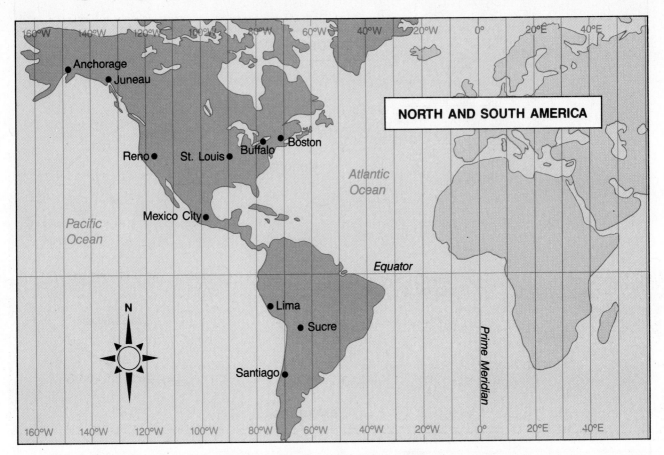

1. Are North and South America east or west of the Prime Meridian? _____
2. North and South America are in which hemisphere?

   _____

3. Trace the 150°W meridian in green.

   What city is near 150°W? _____
4. Trace the 120°W meridian in red.

   What city is near 120°W? _____
5. Trace the 80°W meridian in orange.

   What city is nearest 80°W? _____
6. Find Lima in South America. Circle it.

   Estimate the longitude of Lima. _____
7. Find Sucre in South America. Circle it.

   Estimate the longitude of Sucre. _____
8. Find Juneau in North America. Circle it.

   Estimate the longitude of Juneau. _____
9. What city is north of the Equator and near 70°W longitude? _____

Finding Longitude

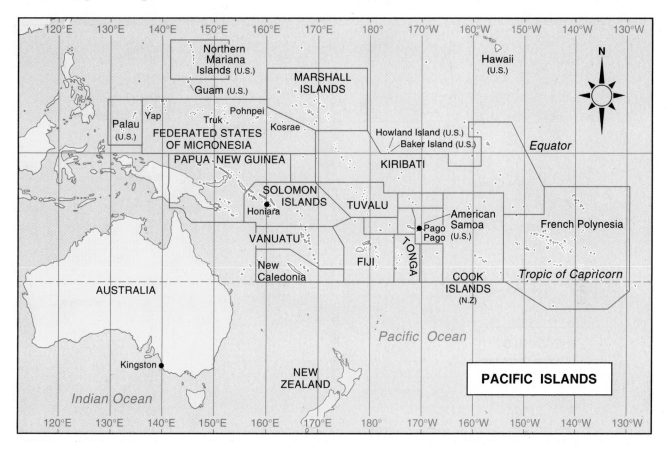

1. Trace the 180° meridian in red.
2. Are the Northern Mariana Islands in the Eastern Hemisphere or Western

   Hemisphere? _____

3. Is American Samoa in the Eastern Hemisphere or Western Hemisphere?

   _____

4. What city is at 160°E? _____

5. In the Federated States of Micronesia, what island is at 138°E? _____

6. What U.S. island lies between 120°E and 140°E? _____

7. What is the longitude of Kingston, Australia? _____

8. Estimate the longitude of Pago Pago. _____

9. Estimate the longitude of Guam. _____

10. Estimate the longitude of Hawaii. _____

11. What two islands are just north of the Equator and at about 176°W?

   _____

Finding Latitude and Longitude

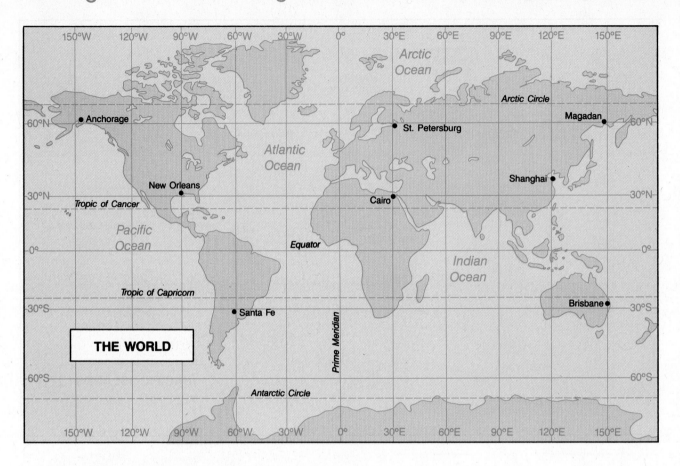

1. Trace the Equator in green.
2. Trace the Prime Meridian in red.
3. Circle the point where the Equator and the Prime Meridian cross.

   Is that point on land or on water? _____
4. Trace the 30°N latitude line in blue.
5. Trace the 90°W longitude line in orange.

6. What city is near the point where 30°N and 90°W cross? _____
7. Trace the 150°E longitude line in purple.
   What two cities lie near this line?

   a. _____ b. _____
8. To locate these cities, you also need to know their degrees latitude.
   Write their degrees latitude after their names in number 7.
9. Anchorage and St. Petersburg are near the same line of latitude.

   What is the line of latitude? _____
10. Anchorage and St. Petersburg are on different lines of longitude. Estimate
    their degrees longitude.

    Anchorage _____   St. Petersburg _____

Skill Check

Vocabulary Check

Prime Meridian   longitude   meridian
Eastern Hemisphere   Western Hemisphere

1. Another word for a line of longitude is a _____.

2. The 0° longitude line is also called the _____.

3. The Prime Meridian and the 180° meridian divide the globe into the

_____ and the _____.

Map Check

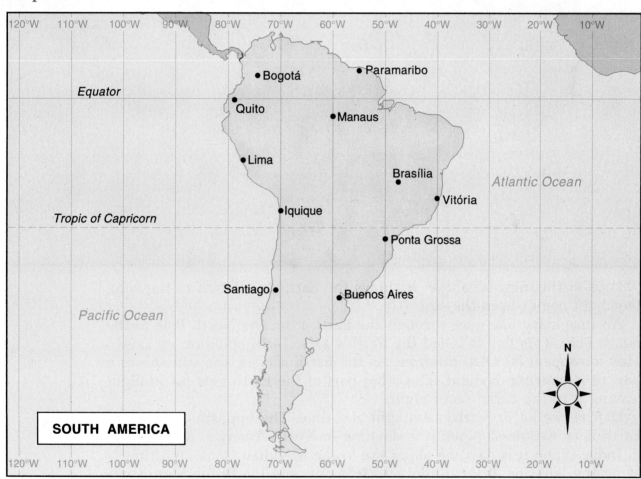

1. Is South America in the Eastern Hemisphere or the Western Hemisphere?

_____

2. What city lies at 40°W? _____

3. Estimate the longitude of Paramaribo. _____

4. What city is south of the Tropic of Capricorn and near 70°W longitude?

_____

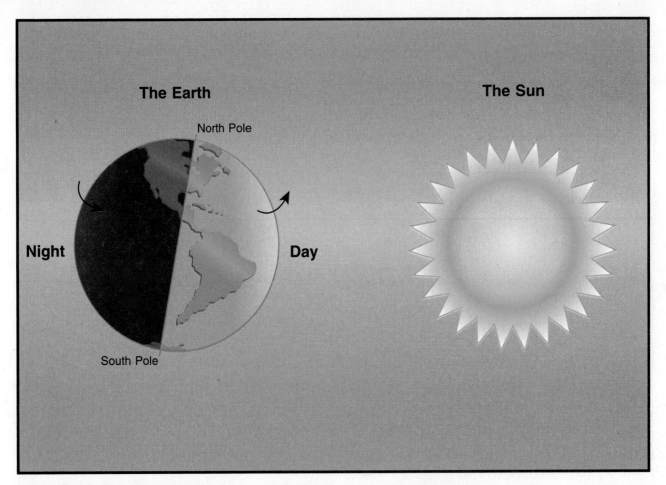

Look at the diagram above. It shows the Earth in relation to the sun. Our light comes from the sun.

An imaginary line goes through the Earth from the North Pole to the South Pole. This line is called the Earth's **axis**. Earth spins on its axis. This movement is called **rotation**. As the Earth rotates, the sun shines on part of it, making daylight. The other part of the Earth gets no sunlight, leaving it in the darkness of night.

Half of the Earth receives sunlight at a time. The opposite half of the Earth is in darkness. When it is daytime in North America, it is nighttime in India. When it is daytime along the Prime Meridian, it is nighttime along the 180° line of longitude, which is opposite the Prime Meridian.

Notice that the Earth is tilted. Areas along the Equator always get about the same amount of sunshine, winter or summer. At the North and South Poles, the amount of sunshine changes with the seasons. For a short time during the year, one pole gets sunshine all 24 hours every day. During this same time, the other pole gets no sunshine.

► If it is day in Europe, is it night or day in Australia?

► If it is day in one place on the Equator, is it day everywhere else on the Equator?

► Who sees the sun first, people in New York or people in California?

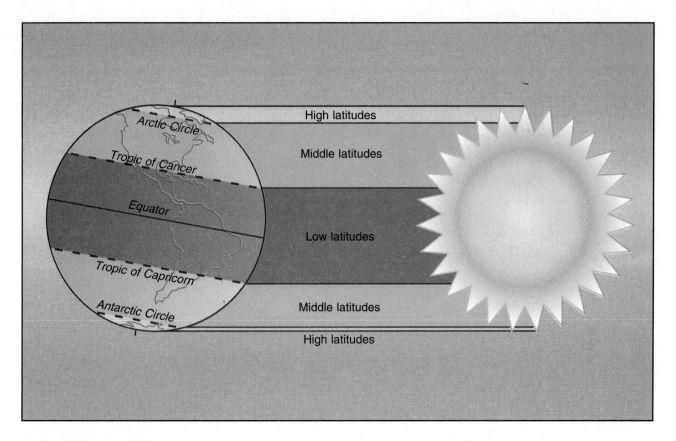

Because the Earth is round, the sun's rays reach the Earth in different ways. The rays are strongest and most direct at the Equator. But at the poles the rays are less strong and direct. Because of this, the Earth is divided into three **climate zones**. **Climate** is the average weather of one place over a long period of time.

Look at the diagram. The area between the Tropic of Capricorn and the Tropic of Cancer receives most of the sun's heat. This climate zone is called the **low latitudes**. Remember that the Equator is 0°. The latitudes close to the Equator have low latitude numbers. Generally the low latitudes have a warm climate.

Look at the areas near the North Pole and the South Pole. These areas receive the least of the sun's heat. They are called the **high latitudes**. The high latitudes are north of the Arctic Circle and south of the Antarctic Circle. Remember that the North and South Poles have the highest latitude numbers—90°. The climate of the high latitudes is usually cold.

Between the high and low latitudes are the **middle latitudes**. The middle latitudes fall between the Tropic of Cancer and the Arctic Circle, and between the Tropic of Capricorn and the Antarctic Circle. The middle latitudes are usually warm in summer and cool in winter.

► Find the high latitudes on the diagram.
  What continents are in the high latitudes?

► Find the middle latitudes on the diagram.
  What continents are in the middle latitudes?

► Find the low latitudes on the diagram.
  What continents are in the low latitudes?

Finish this diagram.
1. Label the sun.
2. Label the Equator.
3. Label the Tropic of Cancer and the Tropic of Capricorn.
4. Label the Arctic Circle and the Antarctic Circle.
5. Label the North Pole and the South Pole.
6. Color the low latitudes red.
7. Color the middle latitudes orange.
8. Color the high latitudes yellow.

9. The North and South Poles are in which climate zone? _____

10. The Equator is in which climate zone? _____

Locating Temperature Zones

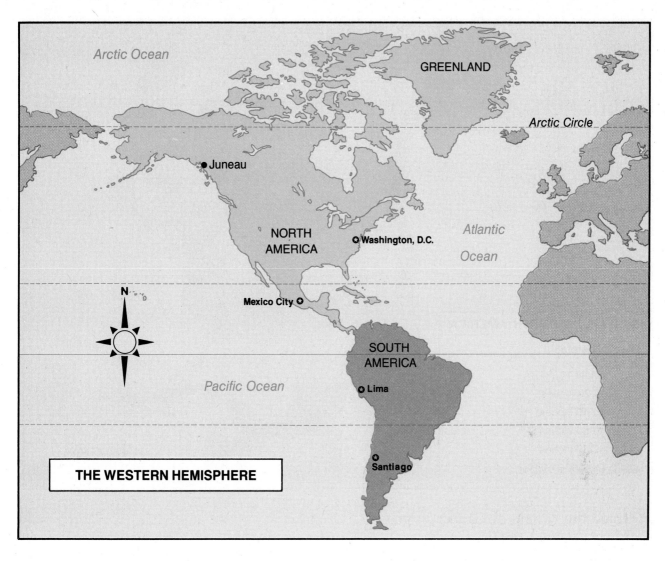

1. Label the Equator.
2. Label the Tropic of Cancer and the Tropic of Capricorn.

3. Greenland is mostly in what climate zone? _____

4. North America is in what three climate zones? _____

   _____ and _____

5. Most of North America is in which climate zone? _____

6. Name two cities in the low latitudes. _____
7. Draw a conclusion. Do you think the climate would be warmer in the
   northern part of South America or in the southern part of South

   America? _____

   Why? _____

Reading a Climate Map

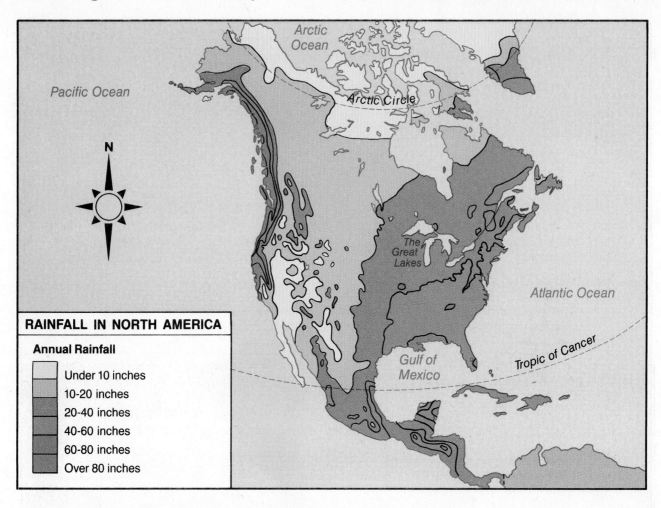

RAINFALL IN NORTH AMERICA

Annual Rainfall

Under 10 inches
10-20 inches
20-40 inches
40-60 inches
60-80 inches
Over 80 inches

1. Trace the Tropic of Cancer in green.

2. Is there more rain north or south of the Tropic of Cancer? _____

3. What climate zone is just south of the Tropic of Cancer? _____

4. Would the weather there be warm and rainy or cold and rainy?

   _____

5. Trace the Arctic Circle in red.

6. Is there more rain north or south of the Arctic Circle? _____

7. What climate zone is north of the Arctic Circle? _____

8. Would the weather there be cold and wet or cold and dry?

   _____

9. Draw a conclusion. Which latitudes in North America would be better

   for growing food, the high latitudes or the low latitudes? _____

   Why? _____

Skill Check

Vocabulary Check   axis   rotation   middle latitudes   climate zone
                        climate   low latitudes   high latitudes

1. The average weather of one place over a long period of time is called

   _____.

2. The Earth spins on its _____.
3. The climate zone south of the Antarctic Circle is called the

   _____.

4. The climate zone between the Tropic of Cancer and the Tropic of

   Capricorn is called the _____.
5. The climate zone between the Tropic of Cancer and the Arctic Circle

   is called the _____.

Map Check

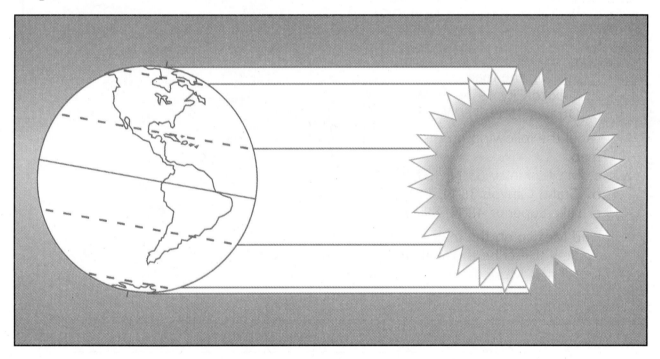

1. Color the high latitudes yellow.
2. Color the middle latitudes orange.
3. Color the low latitudes red.

4. North America is mostly in the _____.

5. The Equator is in the _____.

6. Which climate zone has the coldest weather? _____

Geography Themes Up Close

Location tells where something is found. Every place on Earth has a location. There are two ways of naming a location. **Relative location** tells what it is near or what is around it. **Absolute location** gives the exact location by using latitude and longitude lines.

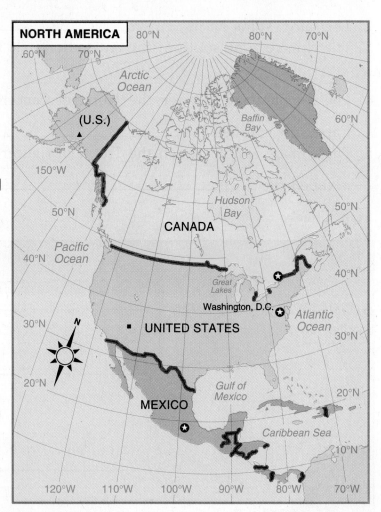

1. Greenland, the largest island in the world, is located northeast of Canada. Greenland is located east of Baffin Bay. Most of Greenland is north of the Arctic Circle. Label Greenland on the map.

2. Label the following national capitals on the map.
   a. Mexico City 19°N, 99°W
   b. Ottawa 45°N, 76°W

3. Label the following on the map.
   a. Mt. McKinley 63°N, 151°W
   b. Grand Canyon 36°N, 112°W
   c. Lake Superior 48°N, 89°W

4. Find Mexico on the map. Circle it. Describe the relative location of Mexico.

_____

_____

_____

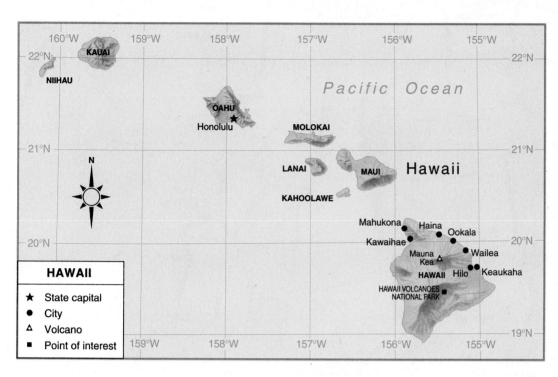

5. Describe the relative location of Honolulu. Explain why its location might be one reason Honolulu was chosen as the capital of Hawaii.

_____

_____

_____

6. What is the absolute location of the volcano Mauna Kea—the highest point in Hawaii?

_____

7. Where are most cities and towns on the island of Hawaii located? Why do you think this is so?

_____

_____

_____

_____

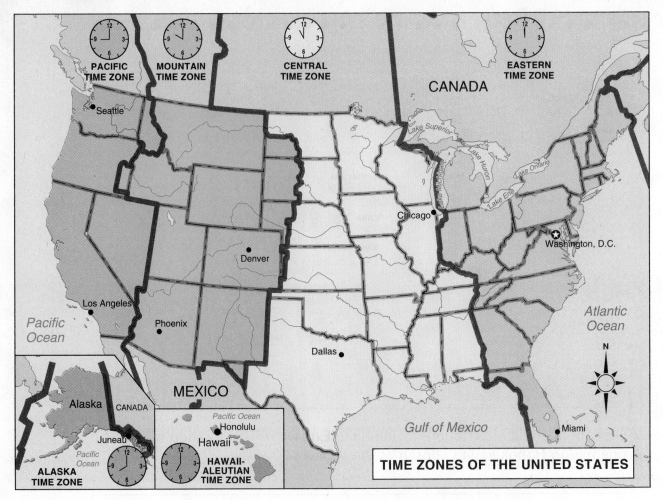

TIME ZONES OF THE UNITED STATES

You know that the Earth is turning all the time. It makes one complete rotation or turn every 24 hours. Remember that the Earth gets its light from the sun. Only half of the Earth receives light at a time. As the Earth turns, one part of the Earth gets lighter while another part gets darker.

It is not the same time everywhere on Earth. The Earth is divided into 24 time zones. There is one time zone for each hour in the day.

Six of the world's 24 **time zones** are in the United States. Look at the time zone map above. The time in each zone is different by one hour from the zone next to it. Washington, D.C. is in the Eastern Time Zone. Chicago is in the Central Time Zone. When it is 8:00 A.M. in Washington, D.C., it is 7:00 A.M. in Chicago. In Denver, which is in the Mountain Time Zone, it is 6:00 A.M. In San Francisco, which is in the Pacific Time Zone, it is 5:00 A.M. In the Alaska Time Zone, it is 4:00 A.M. In the Hawaii-Aleutian Time Zone, it is 3:00 A.M.

► In which time zone do you live?

► How do you think the Pacific Time Zone got its name?

► What mountain range goes through the Mountain Time Zone?

► New York City is in which time zone?

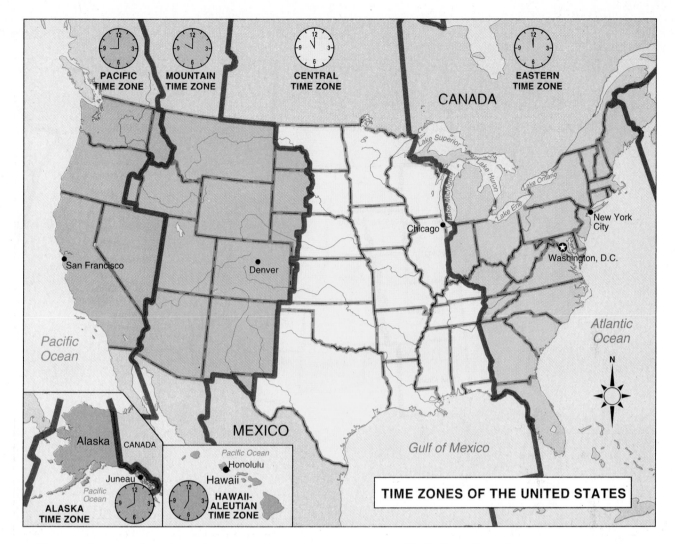

Look at the time zone map above. Put your finger on the Mountain Time Zone. Suppose it is 7:00 there. Move your finger one time zone east, to the Central Time Zone. Add one hour to the time. It is 8:00 Central time.

If you know the time in one time zone, you can find the time in others. If you go east one time zone, add one hour to the time. If you go east two time zones, add two hours to the time. If you go west one time zone, subtract one hour from the time.

Look at the time zone map above. Put your finger on the Mountain Time Zone. Suppose it is 7:00 there. Move your finger one time zone east, to the Central Time Zone. Add one hour to the time. It is 8:00 Central time.

Move your finger back to the Mountain Time Zone. It is still 7:00. Now move your finger one time zone west to the Pacific Time Zone. Remember, you subtract one hour for each time zone you go west.

► What time is it in the Pacific Time Zone?

► Name two cities in each time zone.

► If it is 6:00 in Chicago, what time is it in Washington, D.C.? What time is it in Phoenix? What time is it in Seattle?

► If it is 12:00 noon in Chicago, what time is it in Washington, D.C.? What time is it in Honolulu? What time is it in Juneau?

Reading a Time Zone Map

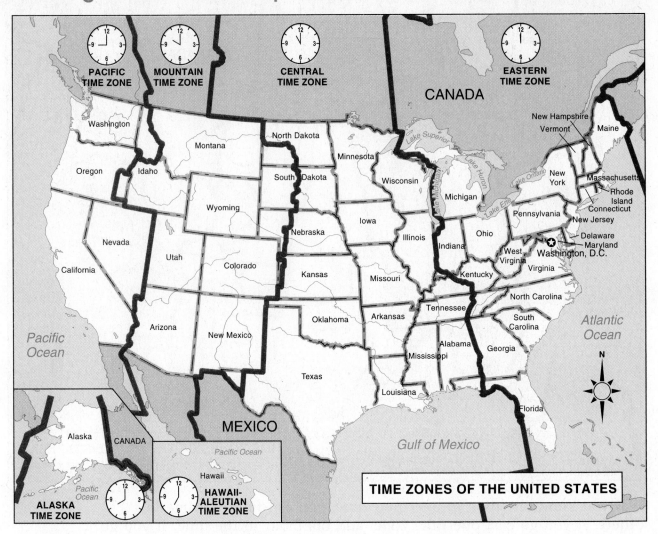

1. Lightly color the time zones. Use a different color for each zone. Notice that the lines are not always straight. Time zones often follow state boundaries or physical features.

2. In which time zone do you find these states?

   California _____   Pennsylvania _____

   Illinois _____   Hawaii _____

3. It is 10:00 A.M. in California. What time is it in Wyoming? _____

4. It is 5:00 P.M. in Georgia. What time is it in Alaska? _____

5. It is 12:00 noon in Illinois. What time is it in Virginia? _____

6. It is 4:00 P.M. in Massachusetts. What time is it in Oklahoma? _____

7. It is 12:00 midnight in Iowa. What time is it in New Mexico? _____

8. It is 4:30 A.M. in Colorado. What time is it in Washington state? _____

Reading a Time Zone Map

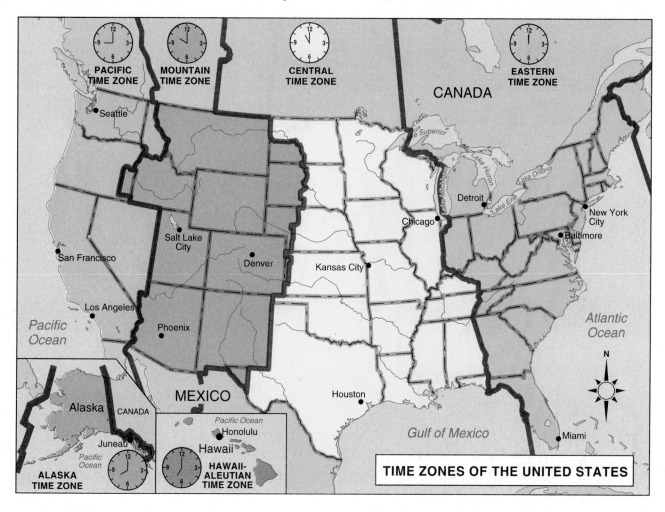

1. It is 7:00 A.M. in Denver. What time is it in the cities listed below?

    Honolulu   _____   Phoenix   _____

    Los Angeles   _____   Miami   _____

    Detroit   _____   New York City   _____

2. It is 12:00 noon in Chicago. What time is it in the cities listed below?

    Juneau   _____   Seattle   _____

    Denver   _____   Baltimore   _____

    Houston   _____   San Francisco   _____

3. The first people to see the sunrise live in the _____ Time Zone.

4. The last people to see the sun set live in the _____ Time Zone.

Reading a Time Zone Map

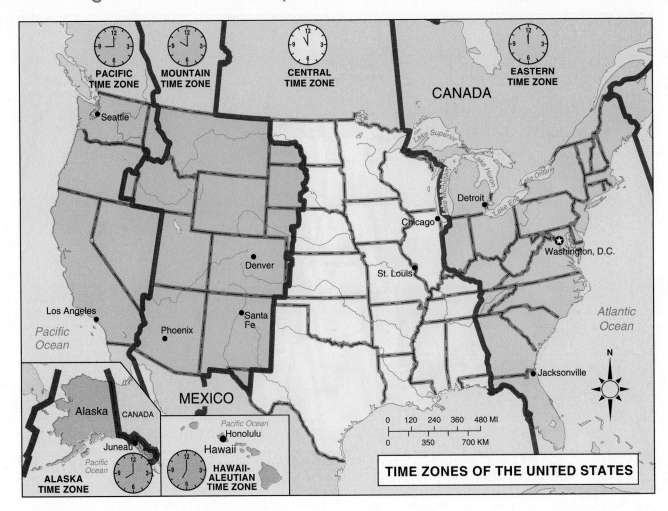

1. You will be traveling to several cities in the United States. Draw a line from

   Jacksonville to St. Louis. What direction will you be traveling? _____
   When you arrive in St. Louis, it is 2:00 P.M. What time is it in

   Jacksonville? _____

2. From St. Louis, you will drive to Denver. Draw a line to connect these

   two cities. From St. Louis to Denver is about _____ miles. What

   direction will you be traveling? _____

3. You will drive from Denver to Los Angeles to visit friends. Draw a line
   connecting these two cities.

   It is 7:00 A.M. in Los Angeles. What time is it in Denver? _____

   What time is it in Jacksonville? _____

Skill Check

Vocabulary Check   time zone

Map Check

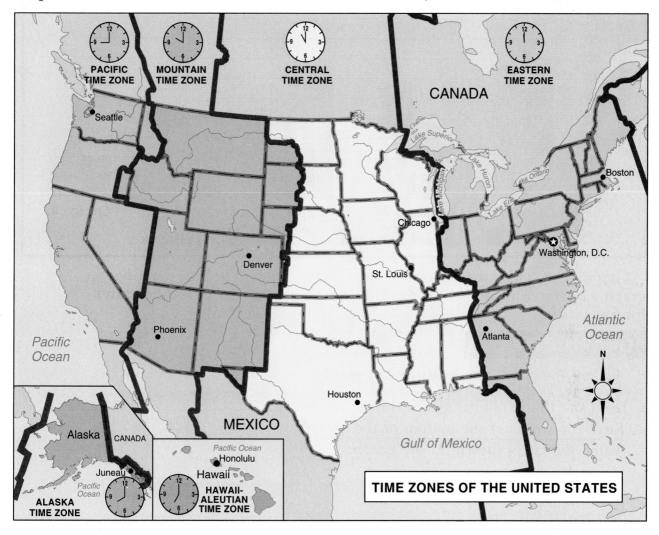

TIME ZONES OF THE UNITED STATES

1. The Earth is divided into 24 _____.

2. Atlanta is in the _____ Time Zone.

3. Phoenix is in the _____ Time Zone.

4. It is 2:00 P.M. in St. Louis. What time is it in the following cities?

   Denver _____   Seattle _____

   Atlanta _____   Honolulu _____

5. It is 12:00 noon in Denver. What time is it in the following cities?

   Houston _____   Seattle _____

   Juneau _____   Washington, D.C. _____

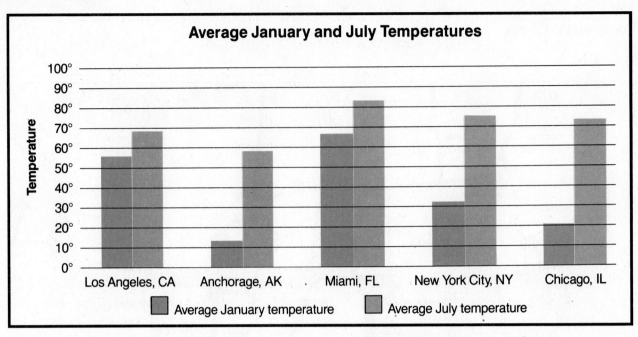

Average January and July Temperatures

Graphs use colors and shapes to show information. The bars on a **bar graph** allow you to compare facts. This bar graph shows two temperatures for five cities.

GRAPH ATTACK!

Follow these steps to read the bar graph.

1. Read the title. This bar graph shows _____.
2. Read the words at the bottom of the graph.
   Name the cities shown on the graph.

   _____

   The green bars stand for _____.

   The orange bars stand for _____.
3. Read the words and numbers on the left side of the graph. The

   numbers on the graph stand for _____.
4. Compare the bars. Put your finger at the top of the first bar for Miami. Slide your finger to the left. Read the number there.

   The average January temperature in Miami is about _____.

   The average July temperature in Miami is about _____.

   Which city has the lowest January temperature? _____
5. Draw a conclusion. Which three cities have the coldest winters?

   _____

Reading a Bar Graph

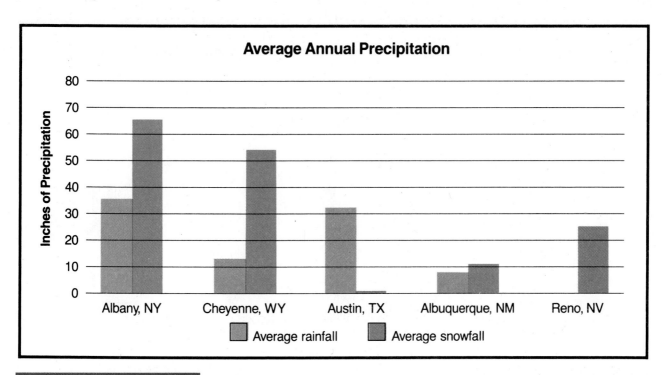

Average Annual Precipitation

Inches of Precipitation

Albany, NY   Cheyenne, WY   Austin, TX   Albuquerque, NM   Reno, NV

Average rainfall   Average snowfall

GRAPH ATTACK!

Follow these steps to read the bar graph.

1. <u>Read the title.</u> This bar graph shows _____.
2. <u>Read the words at the bottom of the graph.</u>

   The brown bars on this graph stand for _____.

   The blue bars on this graph stand for _____.
3. <u>Read the words and numbers at the left side of the graph.</u>

   The numbers on the graph stand for _____.
4. <u>Compare the bars.</u> Use <u>more</u> or <u>less</u> in each sentence.

   Cheyenne receives _____ snow than Albany.

   Austin receives _____ rain than Albuquerque.

   Reno receives _____ snow than Albuquerque.

   Which city receives the most rain? _____

   Which city receives the least snow? _____
5. <u>Finish the graph.</u> Reno, Nevada receives 8 inches of rain. Add a bar showing the amount of rain Reno receives.
6. <u>Draw a conclusion.</u> Which city gets about the same amount of rain

   as snow? _____

Circle Graphs

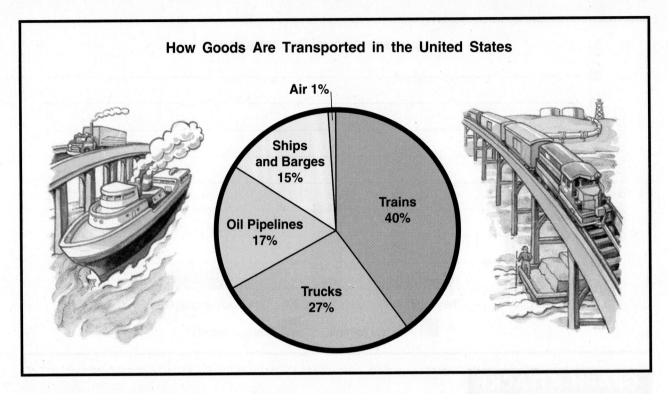

How Goods Are Transported in the United States

Air 1%

Ships and Barges 15%

Oil Pipelines 17%

Trains 40%

Trucks 27%

A **circle graph** shows the parts that make up a whole set of facts. Each part of the circle is a percentage of the whole. All the parts together equal 100%. This circle graph shows the percentage of all goods moved by each method of transportation.

GRAPH ATTACK!

Follow these steps to read the circle graph.

1. Read the title. The whole circle shows _____

   _____ .

2. Read each part of the circle. Each part of the circle stands for a different way of transporting goods. What are the different ways?

   _____

3. Compare the parts. Read clockwise around the circle from the biggest part. Write More or Fewer in each sentence.

   _____ goods are carried by trucks than by ships and barges.

   _____ goods are carried by trucks than by trains.

   _____ goods are carried by trains than by oil pipelines and ships and barges together.

4. Draw a conclusion. What two methods of transportation carry about

   the same amount of goods? _____

Reading a Circle Graph

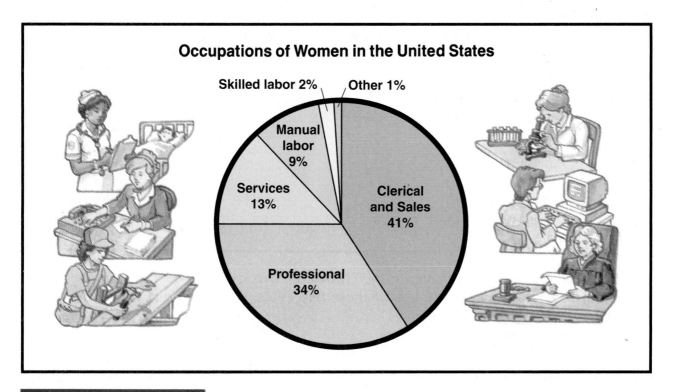

Occupations of Women in the United States

Skilled labor 2% Other 1%

Manual labor 9%

Services 13%

Clerical and Sales 41%

Professional 34%

GRAPH ATTACK!

Follow these steps to read the circle graph.

1. <u>Read the title.</u> The circle graph shows _____
2. <u>Read each part of the circle.</u>

   What percent of women hold clerical and sales positions? _____

   What percent of women hold manual labor positions? _____

   What percent of women hold positions in manual and skilled labor? _____
3. <u>Compare the parts of the circle.</u> Use <u>More</u> or <u>Fewer</u> in each sentence.

   _____ women hold positions in skilled labor than in manual labor.

   _____ women hold professional positions than service positions.

   _____ women hold professional positions than clerical and sales positions.

   Would you be more likely to meet a woman who was a professional or a woman who was in sales? _____
4. <u>Draw a conclusion.</u> Most women work in what three areas?

   _____

Line Graphs

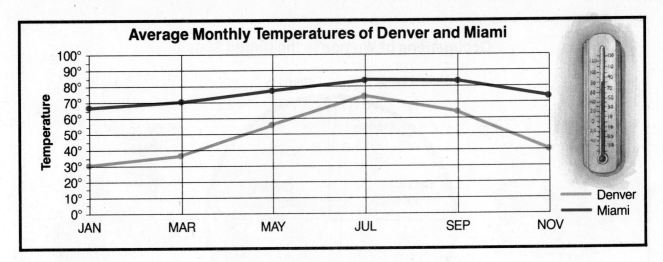

Average Monthly Temperatures of Denver and Miami

Denver
Miami

   Some students wanted to compare the climate of two U.S. cities. They made a line graph to show the temperatures of these two cities. A **line graph** shows how something changes over time.

GRAPH ATTACK!

   Follow these steps to read a line graph.

1. <u>Read the title.</u> This line graph shows _____

   _____ .

2. <u>Read the words along the bottom of the graph.</u>
   This line graph shows the average temperatures for the months of

   _____ .

3. <u>Read the words and numbers on the left side of the graph.</u> These numbers

   stand for _____ . The highest number is _____ .

4. <u>Read the lines on the graph.</u>
   Find the line for Miami. Put your finger on the dot above January.
   Slide your finger to the left and read the temperature.

   In January the average temperature in Miami is about _____ .

   In January the average temperature in Denver is _____ .

5. <u>Compare the lines.</u>

   Which city has the hottest summer temperatures? _____

   Which city has the coldest temperatures? _____

6. <u>Draw a conclusion.</u>

   Which city's temperatures change the least over the year? _____

   How do you know? _____

Reading a Line Graph

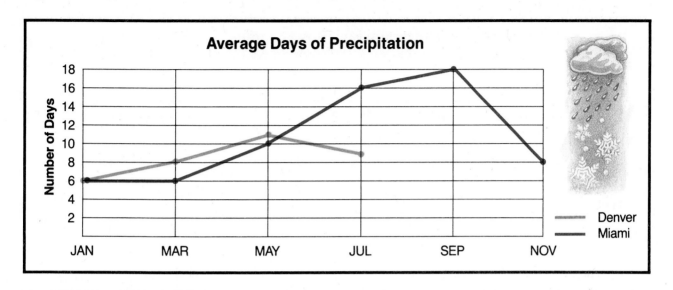

Average Days of Precipitation

Denver
Miami

JAN   MAR   MAY   JUL   SEP   NOV

GRAPH ATTACK!

Follow the first three steps on page 88 to begin reading this line graph.

1. Trace the line for Miami with your finger. Put your finger at the highest point on the line.

   What month does the dot stand for? _____

   How many days of precipitation did Miami have in that month? _____

   How many days of precipitation did Miami have in May? _____
   In what two months did Miami have the same number of days of

   precipitation? _____

2. Finish the graph. Finish the line for Denver. Add dots for this information. Then complete the line.

             September 5 days   November 5 days

3. Compare the lines.

   Which city had more days of precipitation in July? _____

   Which city had more days of precipitation in May? _____

   Which city had fewer days of precipitation in November? _____
   In what month did Miami and Denver have the same number of days of

   precipitation? _____

4. Draw a conclusion. Which city had the biggest change in number of days of

   precipitation overall? _____ How do you know? _____

   _____

Tables

University Hills Bus Schedule
WEEKDAY & SATURDAY SERVICE

OUTBOUND from downtown (Bus sign reads AIRPORT)				INBOUND to downtown (Bus sign reads UNIVERSITY HILLS)			
5th & Congress	9th & Park	12th & Park	Airport & River Road	12th & Park	9th & Park	9th & Capitol	5th & Capitol
7:45	7:53	8:00	8:10	8:17	8:22	8:27	8:35
8:45	8:53	9:00	9:10	9:17	9:22	9:27	9:35
9:45	9:53	10:00	10:10	10:17	10:22	10:27	10:35
10:45	10:53	11:00	11:10	11:17	11:22	11:27	11:35
11:45	11:53	12:00	12:10	12:17	12:22	12:27	12:35
12:45	12:53	1:00	1:10	1:17	1:22	1:27	1:35
1:45	1:53	2:00	2:10	2:17	2:22	2:27	2:35
2:45	2:53	3:00	3:10	3:17	3:22	3:27	3:35
3:45	3:53	4:00	4:10	4:17	4:22	4:27	4:35
4:45	4:53	5:00	5:10	5:17	5:22	5:27	5:35

A **table** shows information using rows and columns. Tables put a large amount of information in a small space. This table is a bus schedule.

TABLE ATTACK!

Follow these steps to read the table.

1. Read the title. This table shows the _____.
2. Read the words at the top of the table.

   Where is the first stop? _____

   When the bus is outbound, what does the bus sign read? _____

   What do the numbers in each column stand for? _____

   On what day could you not ride this bus? _____
3. Read the table. If you caught the bus at 5th and Congress at 9:45,

   what time would you get to Airport and River Road? _____
   If you caught the bus at 12th and Park at 2:17, what time would you

   get to 9th and Capitol? _____
   If you needed to be at the airport at 12:30, what time should you catch

   the bus at 5th and Congress? _____
   If your plane arrived at 2:00, what is the earliest you could arrive at

   5th and Capitol? _____
4. Draw a conclusion. Where does the bus make a loop and head back

   toward downtown? _____

Reading a Table

Road Mileages Between U.S. Cities							
Cities	Birmingham	Boston	Buffalo	Chicago	Cleveland	Dallas	Denver
Boston, MA	1,215	—	461	1,003	654	1,819	2,004
Chicago, IL	667	1,003	545	—	346	936	1,015
Dallas, TX	647	1,819	1,393	936	1,208	—	887
Denver, CO	1,356	2,004	1,546	1,015	1,347	887	—
Detroit, MI	734	751		283	171	1,218	1,284
Kansas City, MO	753	1,427	995	532	806	554	603
Los Angeles, CA	2,092		2,512	2,042	2,374	1,446	1,029
Miami, FL	812	1,529	1,425	1,382	1,250	1,367	2,069
Minneapolis, MN	1,079	1,417	958	409	760	999	924
New Orleans, LA	351	1,563	1,254	935	1,070		1,409
New York, NY	985	215	400	797	466	1,589	1,799
Philadelphia, PA	897	321	414	768	437	1,501	1,744
Salt Lake City, UT	1,868	2,395	1,936	1,406	1,738	1,410	531
San Francisco, CA	2,472	3,135	2,677	2,146	2,478	1,827	1,271
Washington, DC	758	458	384	695	370	1,362	1,686

TABLE ATTACK!

Follow these steps to read the table.

1. <u>Read the title.</u>

   This table shows _____.
2. <u>Read the words at the top of the table.</u> What cities are listed across the

   top? _____
3. <u>Read the words at the left of the table.</u> How many cities are listed? ____
4. <u>Read the table.</u> Put your finger on Boston at the left of the table. Slide your finger to the right until you come to the number under Chicago. Read that number.

   The distance from Boston to Chicago is _____ miles.
5. <u>Finish the table.</u> Add these distances.
   - Detroit to Buffalo   277 miles
   - Los Angeles to Boston   3,046 miles
   - New Orleans to Dallas   525 miles
6. <u>Draw a conclusion.</u> Which of the cities listed is farthest from Dallas?

   _____

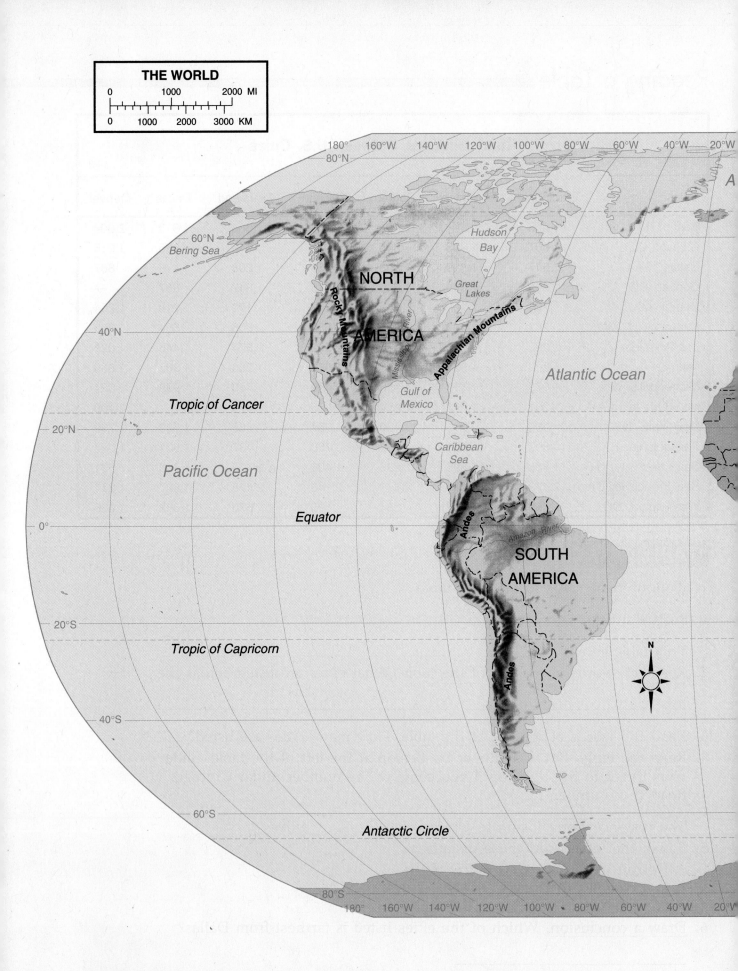

THE WORLD

0   1000   2000 MI

0 1000 2000 3000 KM

180°   160°W   140°W   120°W   100°W   80°W   60°W   40°W   20°

80°N

A

60°N
Bering Sea

Hudson
Bay

NORTH

Rocky Mountains

Great
Lakes

40°N

AMERICA

Appalachian Mountains

Mississippi River

Atlantic Ocean

Tropic of Cancer

Gulf of
Mexico

20°N

Caribbean
Sea

Pacific Ocean

Equator

0°

Andes

Amazon River

SOUTH

AMERICA

20°S

Tropic of Capricorn

N

40°S

Andes

60°S

Antarctic Circle

80°S

180°   160°W   140°W   120°W   100°W   80°W   60°W   40°W   20°

20°E 40°E 60°E 80°E 100°E 120°E 140°E 160°E 180°
80°N

Arctic Circle

Ural Mountains

Ob River

60°N

EUROPE

Volga River

ASIA

Danube River

Black Sea

Caspian Sea

40°N

Mediterranean Sea

The Himalayas

Ganges River

River

Red Sea

Arabian Sea

20°N

AFRICA

Pacific Ocean

Congo River

Nile River

0°

Indian Ocean

20°S

AUSTRALIA

Great Dividing Range

40°S

60°S

ANTARCTICA

80°S

20°E 40°E 60°E 80°E 100°E 120°E 140°E 160°E 180°

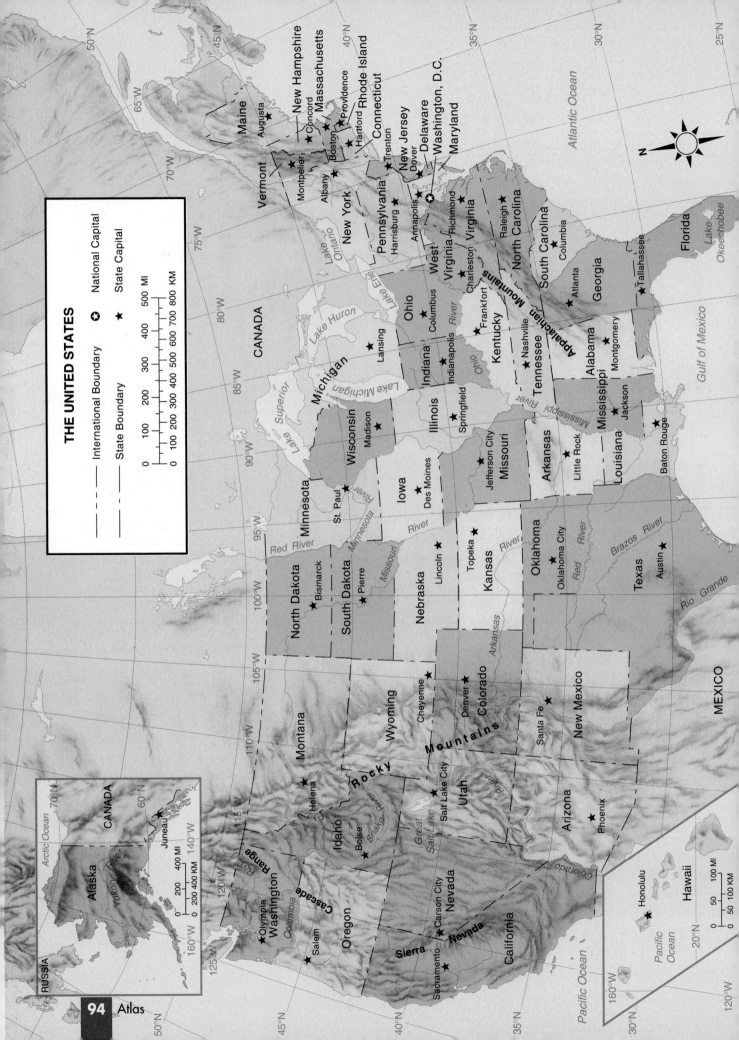

THE UNITED STATES

Legend
- — — International Boundary
- — · — State Boundary
- ✪ National Capital
- ★ State Capital

Scale
- 0 100 200 300 400 500 MI
- 0 100 200 300 400 500 600 700 800 KM

N (compass rose)

CANADA

RUSSIA

MEXICO

Atlantic Ocean

Pacific Ocean

Gulf of Mexico

Arctic Ocean

States and Capitals

Maine — Augusta
New Hampshire — Concord
Vermont — Montpelier
Massachusetts — Boston
Rhode Island — Providence
Connecticut — Hartford
New York — Albany
New Jersey — Trenton
Pennsylvania — Harrisburg
Delaware — Dover
Maryland — Annapolis
Washington, D.C.
West Virginia — Charleston
Virginia — Richmond
North Carolina — Raleigh
South Carolina — Columbia
Georgia — Atlanta
Florida — Tallahassee
Ohio — Columbus
Kentucky — Frankfort
Tennessee — Nashville
Alabama — Montgomery
Mississippi — Jackson
Louisiana — Baton Rouge
Michigan — Lansing
Indiana — Indianapolis
Illinois — Springfield
Wisconsin — Madison
Minnesota — St. Paul
Iowa — Des Moines
Missouri — Jefferson City
Arkansas — Little Rock
North Dakota — Bismarck
South Dakota — Pierre
Nebraska — Lincoln
Kansas — Topeka
Oklahoma — Oklahoma City
Texas — Austin
Montana — Helena
Wyoming — Cheyenne
Colorado — Denver
New Mexico — Santa Fe
Idaho — Boise
Utah — Salt Lake City
Nevada — Carson City
Arizona — Phoenix
Washington — Olympia
Oregon — Salem
California — Sacramento
Alaska — Juneau
Hawaii — Honolulu

Physical Features
- Lake Superior
- Lake Michigan
- Lake Huron
- Lake Erie
- Lake Ontario
- Lake Okeechobee
- Great Salt Lake
- Mississippi River
- Ohio River
- Missouri River
- Minnesota River
- Red River
- Arkansas River
- Rio Grande
- Brazos River
- Red River
- Columbia River
- Snake River
- Colorado River
- Yukon River
- Appalachian Mountains
- Rocky Mountains
- Sierra Nevada
- Cascade Range

Insets
- Alaska — Juneau (CANADA, RUSSIA)
  - Scale: 0 200 400 MI / 0 200 400 KM
- Hawaii — Honolulu
  - Scale: 0 50 100 MI / 0 50 100 KM

Glossary

absolute location (p. 76)   the specific address or latitude and longitude coordinates of a place

acid rain (p. 48)   a kind of pollution that people cause that mixes with water vapor and falls to the ground as damaging rain or snow

Antarctic Circle (p. 57)   the parallel of latitude 66½° south of the Equator

Arctic Circle (p. 57)   the parallel of latitude 66½° north of the Equator

axis (p. 70)   the imaginary line that goes through Earth from the North Pole to the South Pole. Earth spins on its axis.

bar graph (p. 84)   a graph that uses thick bars of different lengths to compare numbers or amounts

cardinal directions (p. 8)   north, south, east, and west

charts (p. 35)   facts shown in columns and rows

circle graph (p. 86)   a graph that shows how something whole is divided into parts

climate (p. 71)   the average weather of a place over a long period of time

climate zone (p. 71)   an area with a generally similar climate

compass rose (p. 9)   a symbol that shows directions on a map

degrees (p. 56)   the units of latitude and longitude lines

elevation (p. 37)   the height of land above the level of the sea

Equator (p. 8)   the imaginary line around the middle of Earth that divides Earth into the Northern and Southern Hemispheres

geography (p. 4)   the study of Earth, its features, and how people live and work on Earth

grid (p. 50)   a pattern of lines drawn on a map that cross each other to form squares

hemisphere (p. 56)   half of a sphere; half of Earth; the four hemispheres are Eastern, Western, Northern, and Southern

high latitudes (p. 71)   the areas north of the Arctic Circle and south of the Antarctic Circle. These areas receive the least of the sun's heat.

human/environment interaction (pp. 5, 62)   the ways that the environment affects people and people affect the environment

human features (p. 4)   features of a place made by people, such as airports, buildings, highways, businesses, parks, and playgrounds

inset map (p. 23)   a small map within a larger map

interdependence (p. 34)   how people depend on one another to meet their needs and wants

intermediate directions (p. 9)   northeast, southeast, southwest, northwest

international boundary (p. 14)   where one country ends and another begins

interstate highway (p. 28)   a main highway that crosses the entire country

kilometers (p. 22)   a unit of length used in measuring distance in the metric system. Kilometers can also be written **KM** and km.

latitude (p. 56)   the distance north or south of the Equator measured in degrees

legend (p. 14)   a map key, or list of symbols on a map and what they stand for

line graph (p. 88)   a graph that shows how something changes over time

location (pp. 4, 76)   the absolute and relative position of people and places on Earth

longitude (p. 64)   the distance east or west of the Prime Meridian, measured in degrees

low latitudes (p. 71)   the area between the Tropic of Capricorn and Tropic of Cancer, which receives most of the sun's heat

map index (p. 51)   the alphabetical list of places on a map with their grid squares

map scale (p. 22)   the guide that shows what distances on a map equal in the real world

meridians (p. 64)   lines of longitude

middle latitudes (p. 71)   the areas between the Tropic of Cancer and the Arctic Circle and Tropic of Capricorn and the Antarctic Circle. These areas are warm in the summer and cool in winter.

mileage markers (p. 29)   small triangles and numbers on a map used to indicate distances along highways

miles (p. 22)   a unit of length that can also be written **MI** or mi

mountain range (p. 36)   a group or chain of mountains

movement (pp. 6, 34)   how and why people, goods, information, and ideas move from place to place

North Pole (p. 8)   the point farthest north on Earth

parallels (p. 56)   lines of latitude

physical features (p. 4)   natural features of a place, such as climate, landforms, soil, bodies of water, and plants and animals

physical map (p. 37)   a map that shows elevation and relief

place (pp. 4, 20)   physical and human features that make a location different from any other

plain (p. 36)   a large area of flat land

political map (p. 15)   a map that shows the boundaries separating states and countries

population map (p. 43)   a map that shows the number of people living in an area

Prime Meridian (p. 64)   the line of longitude from the North Pole to the South Pole and marked 0°. It helps divide Earth into the Eastern and Western Hemispheres.

regions (pp. 7, 29, 62)   places that share one or more features

relative location (p. 76)   describes a location by telling what it is near or what is around it

relief map (p. 36)   a map that shows the land on Earth

resource map (p. 43)   a map that uses symbols to show things in nature that people can use, such as coal, oil, and gold

rotation (p. 70)   the movement Earth makes as it spins around its axis

route (p. 28)   a road or path from one place to another, such as a trail, highway, railroad, or waterway

scenic road (p. 28)   a road that goes through beautiful areas

sea level (p. 37)   the level of the ocean surface

South Pole (p. 8)   the point farthest south on Earth

special purpose map (p. 42)   a map that gives information about a specific subject, such as climate, people, resources, or history

state boundary (p. 14)   where one state ends and another begins

state highway (p. 28)   a main road that connects cities and towns within the boundaries of one state

symbol (p. 14)   a picture on a map that stands for something real

table (p. 90)   a way of showing a large amount of information in a small space, using rows and columns

temperature map (p. 43)   a map that shows temperatures for an area

themes (p. 4)   main topics

time zone (p. 78)   an area on Earth where the time is the same. Earth is divided into 24 time zones.

title (p. 15)   the name of a map

Tropic of Cancer (p. 57)   the parallel of latitude 23½° north of the Equator

Tropic of Capricorn (p. 57)   the parallel of latitude 23½° south of the Equator

Name _____

The map below shows some of the kinds of vacation areas found in the Mountain States.

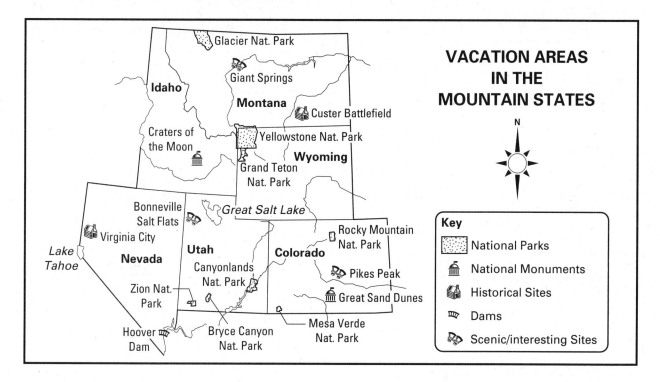

VACATION AREAS IN THE MOUNTAIN STATES

N

Key
- National Parks
- National Monuments
- Historical Sites
- Dams
- Scenic/interesting Sites

1. **In what state is Grand Teton National Park located?**
   - (A) Colorado
   - (B) Idaho
   - (C) Nevada
   - (D) Wyoming

2. **What kind of vacation area is Great Sand Dunes?**
   - (A) Historic site
   - (B) National monument
   - (C) National park
   - (D) Scenic/interesting site

3. **Which type of vacation area covers the most land in the Mountain States?**
   - (A) Historic sites
   - (B) National monuments
   - (C) National parks
   - (D) Scenic/interesting sites

4. **Which national park is located northwest of Yellowstone National Park?**
   - (A) Mesa Verde National Park
   - (B) Canyonlands National Park
   - (C) Bryce Canyon National Park
   - (D) Glacier National Park

5. **What is the name of the scenic/interesting site southwest of the Great Salt Lake?**
   - (A) Bonneville Salt Flats
   - (B) Bryce Canyon
   - (C) Canyonlands
   - (D) Great Salt Lake

6. **Which historical site is located in southeastern Montana?**
   - (A) Yellowstone
   - (B) Giant Springs
   - (C) Custer's Battlefield
   - (D) Craters of the Moon

The maps below show an imaginary country with four states. Use the maps to answer the questions.

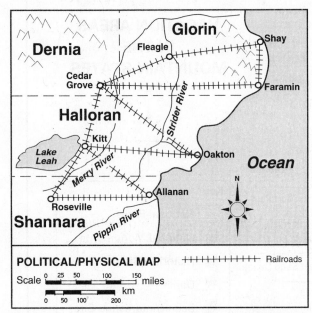

POLITICAL/PHYSICAL MAP   ++++++++++++ Railroads

Scale

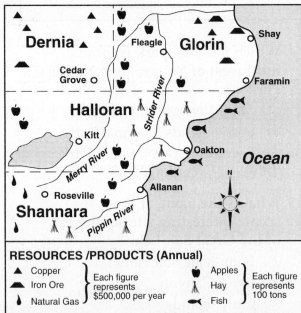

RESOURCES /PRODUCTS (Annual)

▲ Copper
◣ Iron Ore
◖ Natural Gas
} Each figure represents $500,000 per year

🍎 Apples
𝅳 Hay
🐟 Fish
} Each figure represents 100 tons

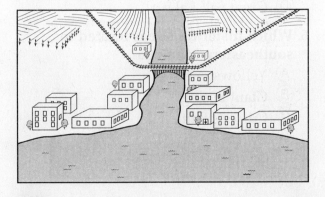

7. The fishing industry is most likely an important part of the economy for which city?
   (A) Shay
   (B) Roseville
   (C) Oakton
   (D) Kitt

8. Which of the following is most likely shipped from Cedar Grove to the coast?
   (A) Fish
   (B) Hay
   (C) Natural gas
   (D) Copper

9. Apples grown in Halloran account for what part of the country's total apple crop?
   (A) 1/3   (C) 2/3
   (B) 1/2   (D) 3/4

10. What else is produced in the hay-and-apple-producing state of Shannara?
    (A) Iron ore
    (B) Natural gas
    (C) Fish
    (D) Copper

11. What is the shortest distance in kilometers by railroad from Cedar Grove to Oakton?
    (A) about 150 kilometers
    (B) about 250 kilometers
    (C) about 275 kilometers
    (D) about 350 kilometers

12. Which city is shown in the picture on the bottom of the left column?
    (A) Oakton   (C) Fleagle
    (B) Faramin   (D) Roseville

Name _____

Use the city grid map below to answer the questions.

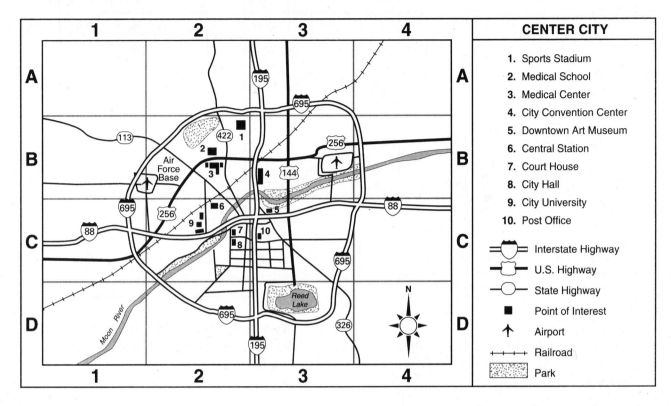

1. **In which grid square is the airport located?**
   - Ⓐ A3
   - Ⓑ B3
   - Ⓒ C2
   - Ⓓ D3

2. **Which two highways meet in the center of the city?**
   - Ⓐ 256 and 88
   - Ⓑ 422 and 113
   - Ⓒ 195 and 88
   - Ⓓ 195 and 695

3. **Which human feature is located in grid square C2?**
   - Ⓐ 195
   - Ⓑ The park along the river
   - Ⓒ The air force base
   - Ⓓ The river

4. **Which highway forms a loop around the city?**
   - Ⓐ 326
   - Ⓑ 422
   - Ⓒ 88
   - Ⓓ 695

5. **Which two buildings are located in grid square C2?**
   - Ⓐ Court House and City Hall
   - Ⓑ Court House and Post Office
   - Ⓒ City Convention Center and Central Station
   - Ⓓ Downtown Art Museum and Central Station

6. **Which is the most direct route from downtown to the city airport in grids B3 and B4?**
   - Ⓐ 256 to 88
   - Ⓑ 195 to 256
   - Ⓒ 88 to 695
   - Ⓓ 88 to 144

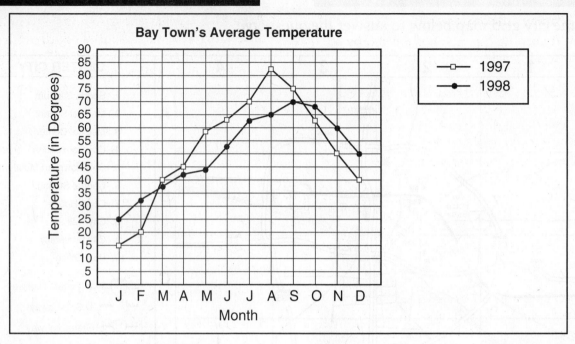

7. **The graph shows the average monthly temperatures in Bay Town for two years. In which year did Bay Town have the hottest summer?**
   Ⓐ 1997
   Ⓑ 1998
   Ⓒ Both years were the same.
   Ⓓ Not enough information is given.

8. **In which year did Bay Town have the coldest winter?**
   Ⓐ 1997
   Ⓑ 1998
   Ⓒ Both years were the same.
   Ⓓ Not enough information is given.

9. **In which month was the average temperature about the same in both years?**
   Ⓐ January
   Ⓑ February
   Ⓒ March
   Ⓓ October

10. **Which month shows the greatest difference in temperature from 1997 to 1998?**
    Ⓐ July
    Ⓑ August
    Ⓒ September
    Ⓓ December

11. **Between which two months did the largest difference occur in 1997?**
    Ⓐ February–March
    Ⓑ April–May
    Ⓒ July–August
    Ⓓ October–November

12. **What other comparison can you make from the information given on the graph?**
    Ⓐ The average temperature for five years.
    Ⓑ The difference in average temperature in 1997 and the previous year.
    Ⓒ The change in average temperature from December 1997 to January 1998.
    Ⓓ The reason for the change in average temperature in each year.

Answer Key

Geography Introduction

Page 4 Location This home is located by a lake near a hill and woods.

Page 5 Place Answers will vary. Students should mention physical features that they can see in the picture, such as trees and a river running through the city. They should also mention human features such as buildings, roads, bridges, parks, and so on.
Human/Environment Interaction In cold weather people wear heavy, warm clothing to keep them warm. In warm or hot weather people wear lighter-weight clothing to keep them cool.

Page 6 Human/Environment Interaction Answers will vary. Students might mention that plants and animal life could be affected by stopping the flow of water in one area and flooding the land in another area.
Movement Question 1. Answers will vary, but may include railways, highways, rivers, airplanes, pipelines, ships, trucks, and so on for people and goods and telephones, telegraphs, newspapers, magazines, radio, television, and so on for information and ideas.

Page 7 Movement Information/Ideas; People/Goods;
Regions The Corn Belt states: Iowa, Illinois, Nebraska, Minnesota, Indiana, Ohio, Wisconsin, Missouri, Michigan, South Dakota. Students should answer that The Corn Belt is a region defined by common land use—the growing of corn.

1 • Directions

Page 8 Question 1. south **Question 2.** north; **Question 3.** west **Question 4.** east

Page 9 Question 1. northwest **Question 2.** southwest **Question 3.** southeast

Page 10 1. Compass rose should be completed. **2.** Kansas should be circled on the map. **a.** Nebraska **b.** Oklahoma **c.** Missouri **d.** Colorado **3.** Wyoming **4.** Mississippi **5.** Missouri **6.** South Dakota **7.** the Pacific Ocean **8.** the Gulf of Mexico

Page 11 1. Compass rose should be completed. **2. a.** north **b.** south **c.** southwest **d.** north **e.** east or northeast **3.** Answers will vary but may include the following: The region is in the northeast corner of the United States.

Page 12 1. Compass rose should be completed. **2.** Hurricane Ridge should be circled. southwest **3.** northwest **4.** south **5.** southwest **6.** west **7.** north

Page 13 Vocabulary Check 1. cardinal directions **2.** North Pole; South Pole **3.** intermediate directions
Map Check 1. Georgia **2.** West Virginia **3.** east **4.** Arkansas; Louisiana

2 • Symbols and Legends

Page 14 Question 1. Answers will vary according to the state in which students live. **Question 2.** Answers will vary according to the state. **Question 3.** Canada and Mexico

Page 15 Question 1. Washington, D.C. **Question 2.** Mexico City **Question 3.** United States **Question 4.** Baja California Norte, Sonora, Chihuahua, Coahuila, Temaulipas

Page 16 MAP ATTACK! Central America **1.** countries; Answers will vary but may include the following: Boundaries are international. Each country has a national capital. Central America is a region consisting of several countries. **2.** Borders of Costa Rica should be traced in red on the map. Nicaragua, Panama **3.** Four capital cities should be added in correct locations. **4.** Guatemala, Honduras, Nicaragua, Costa Rica, Panama

Page 17 1. It is an international border. **2.** Regina should be circled on the map. Regina **3.** Borders of Saskatchewan should be traced in red on the map. Alberta; Manitoba **4.** Ottawa **5.** Nova Scotia **6.** Nunavut **7.** Yellowknife **8.** Whitehorse

Page 18 1. a. Haiti–Port-au-Prince **b.** Dominican Republic–Santo Domingo **2.** Line should be drawn from Nassau to the

bottom of the map. Cuba, Jamaica
3. **a.** northwest **b.** southeast **c.** northeast
4. Caribbean Sea

Page 19 Vocabulary Check 1. political map
2. title **3.** boundaries **4.** legend **5.** symbol
Map Check 1. B **2.** E **3.** A **4.** C **5.** F **6.** D

Geography Feature: Place

Page 20 1. Students should label Big Cypress
Swamp on the map. **2.** Any three physical
features shown the map besides Big Cypress
Swamp: The Everglades, Suwannee River,
lakes, bays, Florida Keys. **3.** Students circle
John F. Kennedy Space Center on the map
and mark with H. **4.** Students label Walt
Disney World on the map.

Page 21 5. Students label the Ottawa River on
map and mark with **P. 6.** Any two of the
following: Mud Lake, Rideau Falls, Rideau
River, Dow's Lake. **7.** Students label Rockcliffe
Airport. **8.** Any two of the following: Supreme
Court, Parliament Building, National Library,
railroad station, Prime Minister's house, City
Hall, University of Ottawa, Museum of
Science and Technology, Ottawa International
Airport, roads. **9.** Answers will vary. Accept
all reasonable answers.

3 • Scale and Distance

NOTE: All distances are approximate.

Page 22 Question 1. miles, kilometers
Question 2. 400 miles

Page 23 Question 1. 240 miles **Question 2.**
900 miles **Question 3.** Alaska is larger than
Hawaii **Question 4.** the United States map
scale **Question 5.** about 220 miles **Question
6.** No, because the space between Honolulu
and Los Angeles is not shown on the maps.

Page 24 MAP ATTACK! Question 1. the
United States **Question 2.** 480
Answers here are approximate.
1. Alaska and Hawaii **2.** 960 **3.** 240 **4.** 1,200
5. 1,000 **6.** Portland to Chicago

Page 25 1. 150 **2.** 150 **3.** 290 **4.** 75 **5.** 525
6. 600 **7.** 300 **8.** 600 **9.** Heron Bay to Cleveland
10. The distances are the same. (Depending on
the points of measurement, one pair of cities
may appear to be farther apart than the other.)

Page 26 1.–5. Lines should be drawn on the
map to connect the places. **1.** Jefferson City
should be circled on the map. **a.** SW **b.** 120
2. **a.** W **b.** 60 **3. a.** SE **b.** 240 **4. a.** N **b.** 140
5. Taum Sauk Mountain should be labeled
on the map.

Page 27 Vocabulary Check 1. miles;
kilometers **2.** inset map **3.** map scale
Map Check 1. 480 **2.** 360 **3.** 840 **4.** Nashville
to Richmond

4 • Route Maps

Page 28 Question 1. interstate highways, U.S.
Highways, state highways, scenic roads
Question 2. Duluth, San Antonio **Question 3.**
Canada **Question 4.** Highway 4 **Question 5.**
in the northern part of the state (7, 23, 27)
Question 6. U.S. 65

Page 29 Question 1. Lake Superior, Lake
Michigan, Lake Huron, Lake Erie **Question 2.**
Pacific States, Southwest, Southeast **Question
3.** Plains States; Southwest **Question 4.**
Interstate 15 **Question 5.** U.S. 83 **Question 6.**
Interstates 90 and 15 **Question 7.** 1122 miles

Page 30 Map Attack! Question 1. the Great
Lakes States **Question 2.** U.S., state, interstate
Question 3. The compass rose should be
labeled with intermediate directions.
1. Minnesota, Wisconsin, Illinois, Indiana,
Michigan, Ohio **2.** Lake Superior, Lake
Michigan, Lake Huron, Lake Erie **3.** The route
should be traced in green to match directions.
29, I-94 **4.** The route should be traced in red
to match directions. 29, 51, 2 **5.** Chicago to
Columbus **6.** in Madison

Page 31 1. the Mountain States **2.** Montana,
Idaho, Wyoming, Nevada, Utah, Colorado
3. The route should be traced in green to

match directions. **a.** I-15 **b.** 482 **c.** Montana, Idaho, Utah **4.** The route should be traced in orange to match directions. I-15, I-90, U.S. 89, U.S. 20, I-25 **5.** U.S. 95 **6.** in Las Vegas

Page 32 Distances here are approximate.
1. Springfield should be circled on the map. Springfield **2.** Chicago should be circled on the map. **3.** 180 **4.** Interstate 55 through Normal; southwest **5.** 90; southwest **6.** 80; northeast **7.** about two hours

Page 33 Vocabulary Check 1. interstate highway **2.** U.S. highway **3.** mileage marker **4.** state highway **5.** region
Map Check 1. I-35 **2.** I-10 **3.** U.S. 70 **4.** I-35 **5.** I-40, I-25, I-10, I-20

Geography Feature: Movement

Page 34 1. Students trace the route on the map. **2.** Atlantic Ocean, Gulf of St. Lawrence, St. Lawrence River, Lake Ontario, Welland Canal, Lake Erie, Detroit River, St. Clair River, Lake Huron, Lake Michigan, Illinois Drainage Canal, Illinois River, Mississippi River **3.** Québec, Montreal, Toronto, Buffalo, Cleveland, Detroit

Page 35 4. Lake Superior, St. Mary's River, Lake Huron, St. Clair River, Detroit River, Lake Erie, New York State Barge Canal, Hudson River **5.** Answers will vary. Accept all reasonable answers. Students might point out that the waterways connect a large portion of both countries making transportation of goods and people possible. **6.** television **7.** Internet, Answers will vary. Accept all reasonable answers. Students might point out that fewer people have access to computers than to the other communication tools shown in the chart, and that not all people who own computers use the Internet.

5 • Physical Maps

Page 36 Question 1. mountains **Question 2.** Answers will vary according to state. **Question 3.** Appalachian Mountains, Rocky Mountains, Sierra Nevadas, Cascade Range, Brooks Range, Alaska Range; Coastal Plains,

Great Plains **Question 4.** Rocky Mountains, because it has the darkest shading **Question 5.** western **Question 6.** plains

Page 37 Question 1. blue **Question 2.** light green **Question 3.** Answers will vary according to region. **Question 4.** blue, purple, dark green **Question 5.** The map colors are the same as the diagram.

Page 38 MAP ATTACK! Question 1. the Mountain and Pacific states **Question 2.** blue **Question 3.** The intermediate directions on the compass rose should be circled.
1. yellow **2.** 500 and 2,000 meters **3.** 2,000 and 7,000 feet; 500 and 2,000 meters **4.** 0 and 700 feet; 0 and 200 meters **5.** Mt. Rainier

Page 39 1. flat **2.** Rhode Island **3.** the White Mountains **4.** Lake Champlain **5.** The Hudson River should be traced; the Atlantic Ocean **6.** 0 and 700 feet; 0 and 200 meters **7.** Answers will vary but may include the following: Hikers would have several changes in elevation, which could be difficult. However, the overall elevation of the mountains is not that great.

Page 40 1. Olympia **2.** 0 and 700 **3.** northeast **4.** About 50 **5.** north **6.** south **7.** Spokane **8.** A line should be drawn between Seattle and Walla Walla. Answers will vary but may include the following: The road would cross rivers at several points and would cover several changes in elevation.

Page 41 Vocabulary Check 1. elevation **2.** mountain range **3.** relief map **4.** plain **5.** physical map
Map Check 1. the Allegheny Mountains **2.** Ohio, Monongahela, and Allegheny **3.** same **4.** Harrisburg **5.** 0 and 1,000 feet; 0 and 300 meters

6 • Special Purpose Maps

Page 42 Question 1. pink; Pacific States, Mountain States, Great Lake States, Plains States, Northeast **Question 2.** along coastlines **Question 3.** Pacific States, Southeast

Page 43 Question 1. purple/blue
Question 2. warm summers and cold winters
Question 3. Alaska: cool summers, cold winters;
Hawaii: warm summers, mild winters
Question 4. cool summers, mild winters
Question 5. Answers will vary according to state.

Page 44 MAP ATTACK! Question 1.
Explorers of North America **Question 2.** Each
symbol should be checked. **Question 3.** The
intermediate directions on the compass rose
should be labeled.
1. Black 2. Spain 3. Hudson **a.** the
Netherlands **b.** 1609 and 1610 **c.** Hudson Bay
or Hudson River 4. DeSoto's route should be
traced in red on the map. Mississippi River
5. Coronado's route should be traced in blue
on the map. Mexico 6. Spain 7. southern

Page 45 1. the population of the United States
2. yellow 3. western 4. dark blue 5. Symbols
should be added to match directions. 6. Any
three are correct: Chicago, Philadelphia, Los
Angeles, and Dallas. 7. New York City

Page 46 MAP ATTACK! Question 1. Land
Use in the Plains States **Question 2.** Each
symbol should be checked. **Question 3.** The
intermediate directions on the compass rose
should be labeled.
1. land use in the Plains States 2. farm land
3. North Dakota 4. Iowa and Nebraska
5. grazing land 6. south 7. Kansas City and
St. Louis should be circled on the map.
a. Kansas City and St. Louis **b.** about
225 miles

Page 47 Vocabulary Check 1. population
map 2. special purpose map 3. resource map
Map Check 1. Arizona and New Mexico
2. Texas 3. Any two are correct: beef cattle,
sheep, fruit, or oil. 4. Arizona 5. Arizona and
New Mexico

Geography Feature:
Human/Environment Interaction

Page 48 1. near Montreal, Lake Ontario, Lake
Huron, Lake Erie, Lake Michigan, Chicago,
Detroit, and Toronto, and in parts of
Michigan, New York, Pennsylvania, West
Virginia, Ohio, Indiana, Illinois, and Kentucky
2. These areas have the least amount of acid
rain. 3. Answers will vary, but students
might answer the northeastern part of the
United States and southeastern part of
Canada, because acid rain levels are highest in
these areas, and pollution from factories helps
cause acid rain.

Page 49 4. All coastal areas of Mexico 5. In
the major cities: Mexico City, Guadalajara,
Monterey, Ciudad Juárez, Veracruz, Tampico,
Chihuahua, Mexicali 6. in southern and
eastern Mexico 7. In areas of little of no
farming 8. Gulf of Mexico because there is
oil there.

7 • Grids
Page 50 Question 1. Chinatown, Afro-
American Museum **Question 2.** Independence
Hall **Question 3.** Fairmont Park; B-2
Question 4. Delaware River; B-6, D-6

Page 51 Question 1. D-2; Court House
Question 2. B-4; northeast **Question 3.** A-1,
A-2; **Question 4.** E-4; Tower of the Americas,
Alamodome

Page 52 MAP ATTACK! Question 1.
Washington, D.C. **Question 2.** The N arrow
on the compass rose should be circled. The
four intermediate directions should be filled
in on the compass rose. **Question 3.** The grid
should be completed with the letters B–D
down the sides and the numbers 2–5 across
the top and bottom of the map.
1. B-2; Item 13 should be circled on the map.
2. C-2; Item 12 should be circled on the map.
Thomas Jefferson Memorial; Lincoln Memorial
or Vietnam Veterans Memorial 3. C-5;
Supreme Court and Library of Congress

Page 53 1. B-6, C-6; First Avenue 2. C-1
and C-2; Line should be drawn to match
directions. Answers will vary but may include
the following; Chrysler Building, Grand
Central Station, or Public Library. 3. B-2;

Route should be traced to match directions. Avenue of the Americas **4.** E-3; Route should be traced to match directions. 34th Street

Page 54 MAP ATTACK! Question 1. San Francisco **Question 2.** The N arrow on the compass rose should be circled. The four intermediate directions should be filled in on the compass rose. **Question 3.** The grid should be completed with the letters B–D down the sides and the numbers 2–4 across the top and bottom of the map.
1. A-1; The Maritime Museum should be circled on the map. **2.** B-2; The Cable Car Museum should be circled on the map.
3. northwest **4.** The cable car route should be traced on the map. east **5.** Interstate 80 **6.** U.S. 101

Page 55 Vocabulary Check 1. grid **2.** map index
Map Check 1. Grid should be completed by adding missing numbers and letters B–F down the sides and 2–7 across the top and bottom of the map. **2.** C-5; City Hall should be circled on the map. **3.** B-6; northeast **4.** D-7; southeast **5.** E-6; southeast

8 • Latitude
Page 56 Question 1. North America **Question 2.** South America **Question 3.** no; North America, Asia

Page 57 Question 1. North America, Africa, Asia **Question 2.** Pacific, Atlantic, Indian **Question 3.** North America, Europe, Asia **Question 4.** Antarctica **Question 5.** Answers will vary depending on location.

Page 58 1.–4. Four lines should be traced to match directions. **1.** Northern Hemisphere; Nome **2.** Southern Hemisphere; Atlantic and Pacific **3.** Northern Hemisphere; Havana **4.** Southern Hemisphere; São Paulo

Page 59 1. Quito **2.** Havana **3.** São Paulo **4.** Santiago de Cuba **5.** Panama City **6.** Sucre **7.** Porto Alegre **8.** 15°N or 16°N **9.** 5°N or 6°N **10.** 34°S or 35°S

Page 60 1. New Orleans and Houston **2.** Denver and Indianapolis **3.** Winnipeg **4.** the Arctic circle **5.** Fort Good Hope **6.** 45°N **7.** 34°N or 35°N **8.** the U.S.-Canada border **9.** north

Page 61 Vocabulary Check 1. parallel **2.** degrees
Map Check 1. The Northern Hemisphere and the Southern Hemisphere should be labeled on the map. **2.** Antarctic Circle **3.** Tropic of Cancer **4.** Fort Smith and St. Petersburg **5.** Iquique and Bowen **6.** Morelia and Nãsik **7.** 0°

Geography Feature: Regions
Page 62 1. They are located along or near water. **2.** about 700 miles **3.** Vancouver, Seattle, Portland

Page 63 4. Students should label Garden District in grid square D-3. **5.** The neighborhood has a view of Lake Pontchartrain. **6.** Answers will vary, but students might point out that French culture or style would be found there in homes and buildings, in food, and so on. **7.** Answers will vary, but students might point out that these regions can then be used as fire districts, police districts, school districts, or local government districts.

9 • Longitude
Page 64 Question 1. Europe, Africa, Antarctica **Question 2.** Europe, Africa, Asia, Antarctica, Arctic, Atlantic, Pacific, Indian **Question 3.** North America, South America, Antarctica, Arctic, Atlantic, Pacific **Question 4.** South America, Antarctica **Question 5.** Africa, Asia, Europe, Antarctica

Page 65 Question 1. Arctic, Atlantic **Question 2.** Pacific, Arctic **Question 3.** Europe, Africa, Antarctica **Question 4.** North America, South America, Antarctica **Question 5.** Earth is round. The curved lines show the spherical shape on a flat surface.

Page 66 1. west **2.** Western Hemisphere **3.–8.** Three meridians should be traced and three cities should be circled on the map to match directions. **3.** Anchorage **4.** Reno **5.** Buffalo **6.** 75°W **7.** 65°W **8.** 135°W **9.** Boston

Page 67 1. The 180° meridian should be traced in red on the map. **2.** Eastern Hemisphere **3.** Western Hemisphere **4.** Honiara **5.** Yap **6.** Palau **7.** 140° E **8.** 170°W **9.** 144°E or 145°E **10.** 155°W **11.** Howland Island and Baker Island

Page 68 1.–5. and 7. Map should be marked to match directions. **3.** water **6.** New Orleans **7. and 8. a.** Magadan–60°N **b.** Brisbane–28°S or 29°S **9.** 60°N **10.** Anchorage–148°W or 149°W; St. Petersburg–30°E or 31°E

Page 69 Vocabulary Check 1. meridian **2.** Prime Meridian **3.** Eastern Hemisphere, Western Hemisphere **Map Check 1.** Western Hemisphere **2.** Vitória **3.** 55°W **4.** Santiago

10 • The Earth and the Sun

Page 70 Question 1. day **Question 2.** no **Question 3.** people in New York

Page 71 Question 1. North America, Antarctica **Question 2.** North America, South America **Question 3.** North America, South America

Page 72 1.–8. Diagram should be finished to match directions with eight labels and three colors. **9.** high latitudes **10.** low latitudes

Page 73 1. and 2. Three parallels should be labeled on the map to match directions. **3.** high latitudes **4.** low latitudes, middle latitudes, high latitudes **5.** middle latitudes **6.** Mexico City, Lima **7.** the northern part of South America; It is in the low latitudes. It is closer to the Equator.

Page 74 1. The Tropic of Cancer should be traced in green on the map. **2.** south **3.** low latitudes **4.** warm and rainy **5.** The Arctic Circle should be traced in red on the map. **6.** south **7.** high latitudes **8.** cold and dry

9. low latitudes; Answers will vary but may include the following: High latitudes are too cold and dry for growing food or low latitudes have warmer temperatures and more rain.

Page 75 Vocabulary Check 1. climate **2.** axis **3.** high latitudes **4.** low latitudes **5.** middle latitudes
Map Check 1.–3. Three colors should be added to match directions. **4.** middle latitudes **5.** low latitudes **6.** high latitudes

Geography Feature: Location

Page 76 1. Label Greenland on the map. **2.** Label Mexico City and Ottawa on the map. **3.** Label Mt. McKinley, Grand Canyon and Lake Superior on the map. **4.** South of the United States, between the Pacific Ocean and the Gulf of Mexico

Page 77 5. It is on the middle island which would make its location central to the rest of the islands. **6.** 20°N, 155°W **7.** near the ocean, along the coast. Answers may vary, but students might point out that the coast gives easy access to water travel, fish and seafood offer a food source, and Hawaii is rugged and made up of volcanic mountains.

11 • Time Zones

Page 78 Question 1. Answers will vary according to location **Question 2.** The zone borders the Pacific Ocean. **Question 3.** Rocky Mountains **Question 4.** Eastern

Page 79 Question 1. 6:00 **Question 2.** Pacific: Seattle, Los Angeles; Mountain: Denver, Phoenix; Central: Chicago, Dallas; Eastern: Washington, D.C., Miami **Question 3.** 7:00; 5:00; 4:00 **Question 4.** 1:00 P.M. 8:00 P.M.; 9:00 P.M.

Page 80 1. Four time zones should be colored to match directions. **2.** California–Pacific; Illinois–Central; Pennsylvania–Eastern; Hawaii–Hawaii-Aleutian **3.** 11:00 A.M. **4.** 1:00 P.M. **5.** 1:00 P.M. **6.** 3:00 P.M. **7.** 11:00 P.M. **8.** 3:30 A.M.

Page 81 **1.** Honolulu–4:00 A.M.; Los Angeles–6:00 A.M.; Detroit–9:00 A.M.; Phoenix–7:00 A.M.; Miami–9:00 A.M.; New York City–9:00 A.M. **2.** Juneau–9:00 A.M.; Denver–11:00 A.M.; Houston–12:00 noon; Seattle–10:00 A.M.; Baltimore–1:00 P.M.; San Francisco–10:00 A.M. **3.** Eastern **4.** Hawaii-Aleutian

Page 82 **1.-3.** Draw lines to connect the four cities. **1.** northwest; 3:00 P.M. **2.** 850; west; **3.** 10:00 A.M.; 8:00 A.M.

Page 83 **Map Check 1.** time zones **2.** Eastern **3.** Mountain **4.** Denver–1:00 P.M.; Atlanta–3:00 P.M.; Seattle–12:00 noon; Honolulu–10:00 A.M. **5.** Houston–1:00 P.M.; Juneau–10:00 A.M.; Seattle–11:00 A.M.; Washington, D.C.–2:00 P.M.

12 • Graphs

Page 84 **1.** average January and July temperatures **2.** Los Angeles, Anchorage, Miami, New York City, Chicago; average January temperature; average July temperature **3.** temperature **4.** 67°; 83°; Anchorage **5.** Anchorage, New York City, and Chicago

Page 85 **1.** average annual precipitation **2.** average rainfall; average snowfall **3.** inches of precipitation **4.** less; more; more; Albany; Austin **5.** Bar for Reno should be added to match directions. **6.** Albuquerque

Page 86 **1.** how goods are transported in the United States **2.** trains, trucks, oil pipelines, ships and barges, and air **3.** More; Fewer; Fewer **4.** oil pipelines and ships and barges

Page 87 **1.** occupations of women in the U.S. **2.** 41%; 9%; 11% **3.** Fewer; More; Fewer, in

sales **4.** clerical and sales, professional, and service

Page 88 **1.** average monthly temperatures of Denver and Miami **2.** January, March, May, July, September, and November **3.** temperature; 100° **4.** 67°; 30° **5.** Miami; Denver **6.** Miami; Answers will vary but may include the following: Denver's temperatures fluctuate more with the seasons than Miami's. Or Miami's line is flatter. Or Miami's line does not change as much as Denver's.

Page 89 **1.** September; 18; 10; January and March **2.** Graph for Denver should be completed to match directions. **3.** Miami; Denver; Denver; January **4.** Miami; Answers will vary but may include the following: The line for Miami shows a greater difference in the number of days of precipitation than the line for Denver.

Page 90 **1.** University Hills bus schedule **2.** 5th and Congress; Airport; time of day; Sunday **3.** 10:10; 2:27; 11:45; 2:35 **4.** at Airport and River Road

Page 91 **1.** road mileages between U.S. cities **2.** Birmingham, Boston, Buffalo, Chicago, Cleveland, Dallas, Denver **3.** 15 **4.** 1,003 **5.** Three numbers should be added to the table to match directions. **6.** ~~Boston~~ *San Francisco*

Sample Standardized Test • Book 2
Page 97 **1.** D **2.** B **3.** C **4.** D **5.** A **6.** C

Page 98 **7.** C **8.** D **9.** A **10.** B **11.** D **12.** A

Page 99 **1.** B **2.** C **3.** B **4.** D **5.** A **6.** B

Page 100 **7.** A **8.** A **9.** C **10.** B **11.** A **12.** C

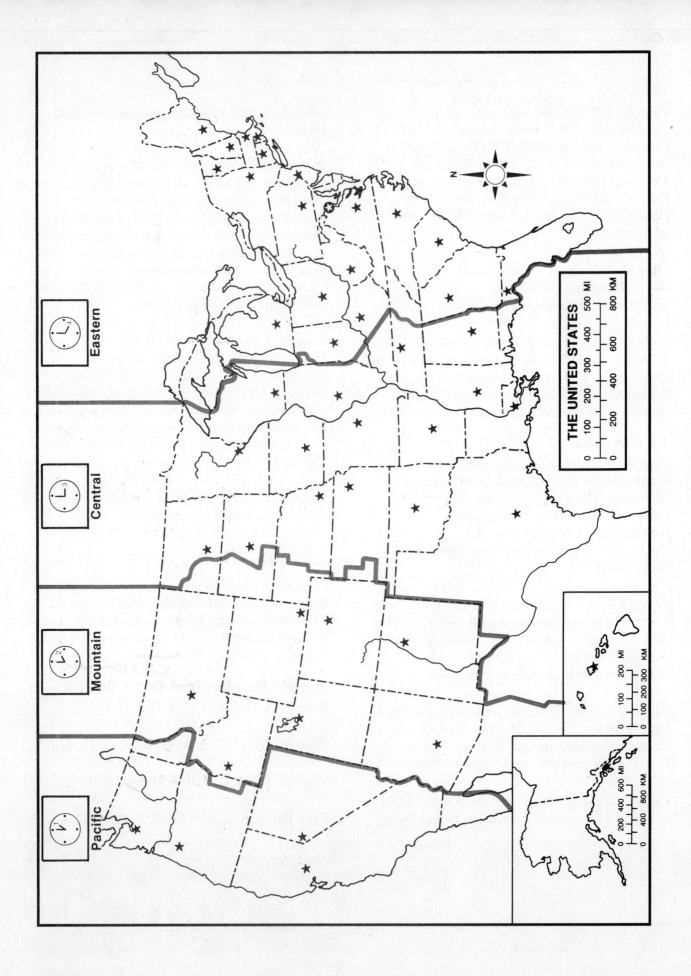

Eastern

Central

Mountain

Pacific

THE UNITED STATES

N

MI
KM

Maps•Globes•Graphs Book 2   © 2000 Steck-Vaughn Company

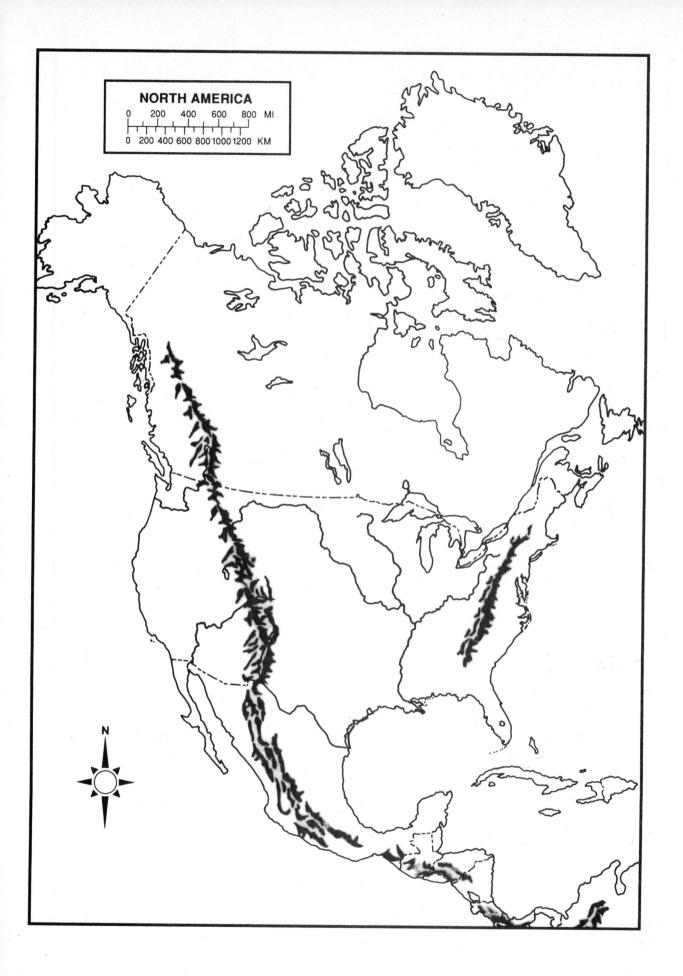

NORTH AMERICA

0   200   400   600   800 MI

0 200 400 600 800 1000 1200 KM

N

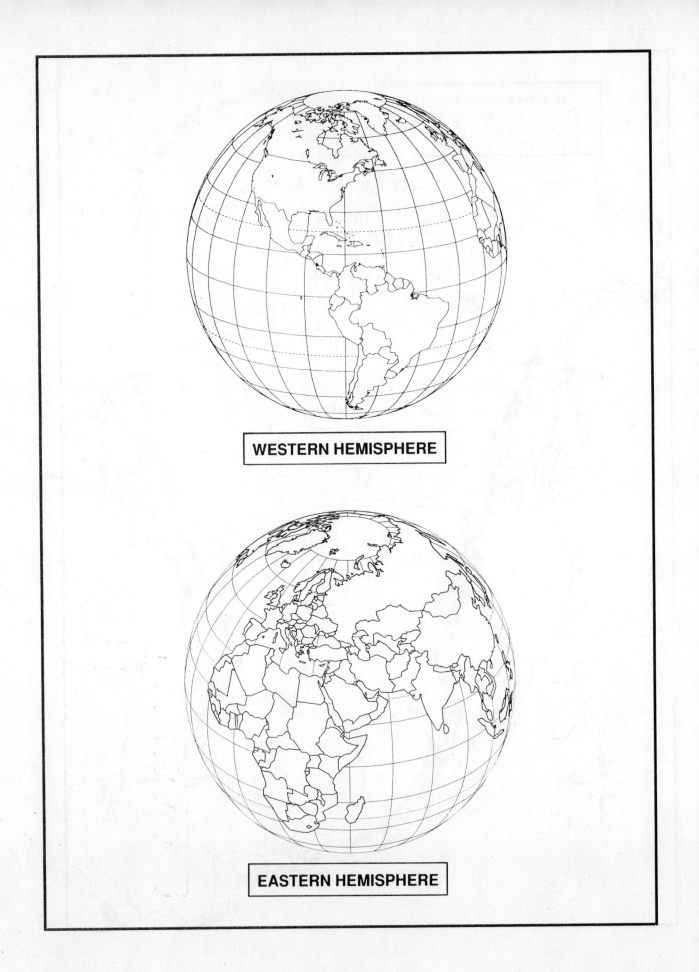

WESTERN HEMISPHERE

EASTERN HEMISPHERE

Maps•Globes•Graphs Book 2 © 2000 Steck-Vaughn Company

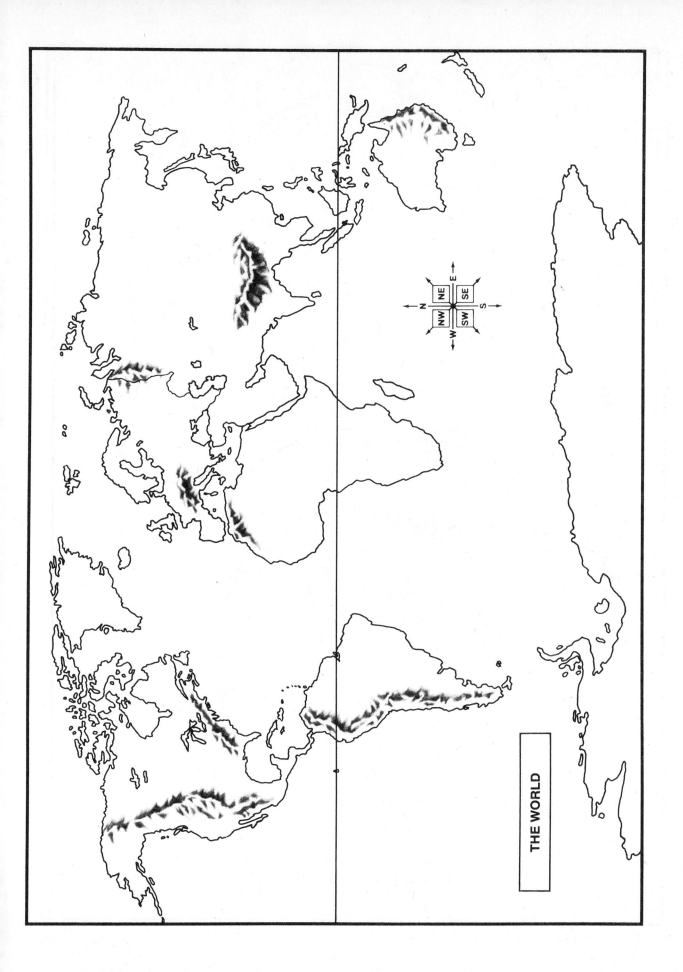

THE WORLD

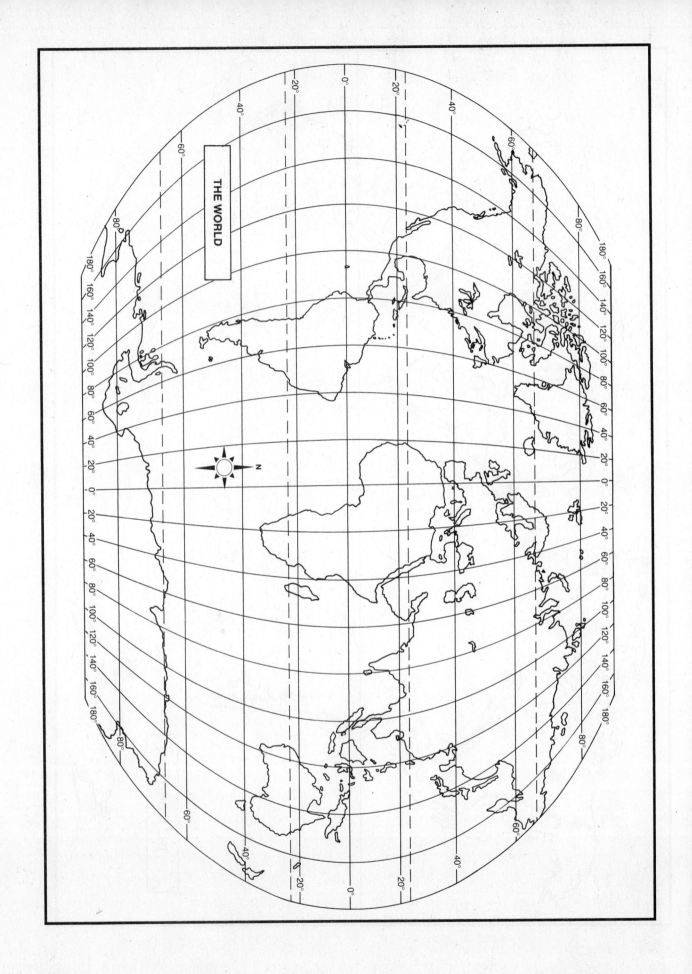

THE WORLD